Baby Not On Board

Baby Not On Board

a Celebration of Life Without Kids

By Jennifer L. Shawne

Illustrations by Anoushka Matus

CHRONICLE BOOKS

SAN FRANCISCO

Library of Congress Cataloging-in-Publication Data available.

ISBN: 0-8118-4797-7

Manufactured in Canada.
Design by Julie Vermeer

Distributed in Canada by Raincoast Books
9050 Shaughnessy Street
Vancouver, British Columbia V6P 6E5

10   9   8   7   6   5   4   3   2   1

Chronicle Books LLC
85 Second Street
San Francisco, California 94105

www.chroniclebooks.com

ACKNOWLEDGMENTS

MANY PARENTS AND UNPARENTS contributed to the content of this book. Although there is not room to thank everyone, I would like to acknowledge Jeffrey and Cathleen Chua Schulte, who make parenting seem almost (dare I say it?) enjoyable; Colin Berry and Blaed Kristin Spence, who know what they're here on earth for and raising babies isn't it; Eric Salmon and Amy "Cool Aunt" Chapman, residents of one of the least childproofed homes in the world, as the death of beloved Mr. Pinchy proved; Robin "they kinda look like aliens" Goddard for her friendship and moral support; dog-baby comparison experts and comic geniuses Stephan Cox and Lori Culwell; the lovely Rosemary Pepper for kindly alerting me to important childfree developments in the news; Brian Misso and Ken Swyt, neither of whom will ever be a protagonist in *My Two Daddies*; Alison Bing, for listening; Marco Flavio Marinucci, for keeping me well fed; and photographer Julian Cash for capturing my playful side.

EVERYONE AT CHRONICLE BOOKS has been incredibly supportive and helpful throughout this process. Special thanks to my editor, Mikyla Bruder, for making this a truly rewarding collaborative effort. This book is much better for her ideas and insights. My appreciation also goes out to Leslie Davisson for her hard work and enthusiasm throughout this project.

SPECIAL THANKS TO MY HUSBAND, ALAN, for putting up with my frequent waffling and freaking out on the subject of procreation. Kudos to our small multitude of nephews and nieces—C.J., Sam, Grace, Kate, Jack, Sophie, and Anna (phew!)—who make being Cool Aunt and Uncle so much fun, and to our parents Will, Kathy, and Sandy, for not pressuring us to supply them with grandchildren.

Table of Contents

Introduction

Congratulations are in order!

THE DECISION not to have children is never an easy one, but now that you've made it, feel free to commence celebrating. Because while new parents' happiest day may be the day their child was born, for you it's the day your child isn't born.

HEY, THAT'S EVERY DAY!

SO, CONGRATULATIONS! Welcome to the club! This book will guide you through what to expect when you're not expecting—from confirming your childfree status and communicating the big news, to the many lifestyle and career benefits your unencumbered state confers. You'll find practical advice on making the most of life in *their* world, appropriate ways to deal with OPCs (Other People's Children), even nonreproductive means of passing along your DNA. Helpful tips and ideas cover a wide range of hot unparenting topics, including how to

convince your baby-lovin' mate that three's a crowd, adopt a delightful child substitute, and ditch pals who turn into scary Zombie Parents. All of this is served with a generous helping of fun. After all, what could be more enjoyable than waking up late on a Saturday morning and realizing you've got nothing to do and nobody to look after other than your sassy little self? Nothing. That's what.

YEAH, THERE'S SOME making fun of babies and parents in this book, too. They're such easy targets, who could resist? What you won't find, though, is any mean-spiritedness. Without kids screaming in their ears all day and emptying their wallets, childfree folks really have very little to be nasty about.

SO, ARE YOU READY to start making the most of life without baby? What are you waiting for? Turn the page!

We're so happy for us!

BABY **NOT** ON BOARD

Guess What?!

Sharing the big news

CHOOSING NOT TO have children is one of the most important and exciting choices you will make in life, and it's certainly one you'll want to share with the people closest to you once the decision is final. In most cases, your announcement will be greeted with squeals of delight, tears of joy, and congratulatory champagne toasts. Alas, a handful of people may cling to the outdated notion that having kids is right and good, while not having them is flat-out freaky.

IF YOU DON'T WANT to let a few misguided fuddy-duddies spoil your happiness, you're going to have to embrace your childfree persona. Come out with a shout, not a whisper. You have a lot to celebrate! By saying "no" to offspring, you are saying "yes" to living your own life to the fullest. And you're in good company, as the list of childfree heroes in this chapter proves. Like Oprah and Dr. Seuss, your sunny outlook is sure to impress even the biggest skeptics. Who knows? You may become the inspiration for a whole generation of unparents!

Are You Really Ready to Announce?

Once you've told people that you're not having children, it can be awkward and embarrassing to change your mind, so you'll want to be absolutely sure of your choice before sharing the happy news. This quiz is designed to help you determine whether you should tell the world or keep it secret for a little while longer. The good news is there's no rush. In fact, taking your time —say three months—will help you solidify your decision and spare you a humiliating about-face later on.

1 *Your tubes are:*

A) Tied.

B) Retired.

C) Flowing with fertility.

2 *How long have you known you didn't want to have children?*

A) Since I was a zygote.

B) Since last week, when that screaming sprog in the supermarket bit my leg.

C) It's not that I don't want to have children . . .

3 *Have you ever "forgotten" to use birth control?*

A) Never! What a ridiculous question!

B) Yes, the scariest day of my life.

C) Oops, I did it again.

4 *Your co-worker wheels his darling little whippersnapper into the office. Where are you?*

A) Cowering under your desk. Won't somebody please make it stop?

B) Headphones on, volume up, eyes tightly affixed to the monitor.

C) Cooing in a clump with the rest of the baby-lovers.

5 *If you were to tell your closest gal pal, "I'm having a baby!" how might she respond?*

A) Five minutes later, she might be able to stop laughing.

B) "What, have you lost your mind?"

C) "One of us! One of us! Gooble gobble!"

6 *How many doors does your car have?*

A) Car? What is "car"?

B) 2—5

C) 6+

7 *What would it take to childproof your home?*

A) A tornado, for starters.

B) A crackerjack team of experts.

C) Foam padding on a few sharp edges, et voilà!

8 *In your daydreams about having a child (however rare), to which of the following is your progeny most similar?*

A) Rosemary's baby

B) Urkel

C) Mini-Me

9 *Are you currently raising a dog or other "child substitute"? (For examples, see pages 124–29.)*

A) No way! Dogs are almost as much work as kids.

B) No, but I'd like to someday. A friendly pup is a perfectly good alternative to a baby.

C) Yes, and I'd love to have more. I'm a born nurturer.

SCORING: Give yourself one point for every A answer, two points for every B answer, and three points for every C answer. Write your total here._____
Now complete the following section.

Give yourself one point if you've publicly used any of the following words to describe someone's baby:

A) Devil Spawn

B) Parasite

C) Brat

D) Monster

E) Poop Factory

F) Yard Ape

Subtract a point for each of the following that you can identify*:

A) Tinky-Winky, Po, Laa-Laa, Dipsy

B) "I Like You, You Like Me"

C) Potty Training Awareness Month

D) The name of the machine that makes "diaper sausages"

E) A doula?

Total score:_____

24–33 No doubt about it, you are bursting with unbabyness! So what are you waiting for? Get on the horn and tell everyone the exciting news.

14–23 You're clearly ready to become an unparent. Make preparations to let everybody know. Start by dropping hints, and in a couple weeks share the big news!

4–13 It's not that you'll never be a happy childfree member of society; it's just that there still may be some doubt in your mind. Take some time to evaluate your feelings before you announce.

* **A)** The Teletubbies **B)** Theme song from TV's *Barney* **C)** June **D)** Diaper Genie **E)** Trained labor coach

Embracing Your Childfree Identity

Why should the "soccer moms" and "stay-at-home dads" have all the fun? Once your mind's made up and you've shared the big news, there's nothing stopping you from fully embracing your childfree identity. Perhaps one of these sounds like you.

Political Abstainer

Not having kids isn't simply a lifestyle choice you've made. It's a calling. You know the world is less crowded, the environment is less polluted, and resources are more abundant thanks to people like yourself. Now if only the rest of the baby-loving world would listen! Your slogan: "Make love, not war, and especially not babies!"

Sprog Snob

These so-called cuties can't discuss literature, are too young to appreciate fine wine, won't sit still for opera, and exhibit a clear aversion to bathing. What, pray tell, is the point of having them? Yes, where others see a darling gurgling infant, you see an anklebiter hellbent on destroying your sanity. The only decision to be made in your mind is whether to turn your nose up at children or to look down upon those drooling, poopy blobs.

Cool Aunt/Uncle

You're perfectly willing to discuss the finer points of saltwater taffy, rough-house, and even read a bedtime story to the offspring of friends and siblings, as long as they're inquisitive and well-behaved enough to merit your attention. And the kids? Those with good taste simply adore you. But you know that the best thing about your pint-sized fans is the fact that you can hand them back at the end of the day.

Career Champ

Why struggle to juggle career and family? For you, true balance is picking one and sticking with it—and you've opted for the one that pays. Your resume will never be stained with grape juice or maternity leave. Your annual presentation to the board of directors will not be marred by Johnny's drawings of turtle turds, nor will your ascent to the top be interrupted by the need to go pump breast milk in the women's restroom.

Clerical Celibate

Like the pope or Mother Teresa, you answer to a higher power, and it's not some screaming two-year-old. The path you've chosen is challenging. Like parenting, it requires hardship and personal sacrifice, but your reward is not the love of some snot-nosed infidel but some prime real estate in the Heavenly Gates subdivision of eternity.

Tortured Artiste

Your greatest masterpiece, should you finish it in your lifetime, will not wear diapers or smear wet crackers all over the place—though, you must concede, that might look kind of cool on a canvas. Primary colors? You'd rather die! The only swing set in your life is currently occupied by your wildly oscillating mood, and you're not about to interrupt your whiskey-soaked nights passed staring down the blank canvas in order to burp and feed a helpless, screaming *enfant terrible*.

Waffling Procrastinator

You definitely plan to have kids, right after you get a promotion, go to graduate school, paint the house, get a dog, travel around the world, win the lottery. . . . Then again, why spoil a full, exciting life with a couple of needy brats? To breed, or not to breed. That is the question, and you'll be infertile by the time you can answer it.

Peter Pan

You'd love to have a new playmate around, but phrases like "role model" and "sharing toys" send you soaring off to Neverland. Your parents want to know when you're going to grow up. Your significant other sighs and wonders when you're ever going to "get serious." But who needs to get serious? Without kids around life is just one long, fun game!

D.I.N.K.s
(Double Income No Kids)

You and your partner enjoy everything your breeding counterparts do—two-car garage, sprawling backyard, weekend cabin by the lake—without the downside of having to share it with any underaged interlopers. Your carefree lifestyle leaves the soccer moms seething with jealousy and the family men wishing they could take back their sperm.

Ten Signs You're Not Parent Material

1 You more or less agree with the statement, "Children are better seen and not heard."

2 You wake up in the middle of the night screaming, "No wire hangers!"

3 You indulge a recurring fantasy about "accidentally" sitting on other people's babies. Oops.

4 You'd love to, but won't the dogs get jealous?

5 Dr. Spock is a Vulcan, right?

6 It's a "designer baby" or nothing.

7 You already have a nursery; it's filled with carnivorous plants.

8 After communing with blessed Mother Earth and consulting your friendly neighborhood shaman, you've self-realized that babies will seriously screw with your aura.

9 On a Vegas bender, you sold your biological clock to a pawn shop and never bothered to get it back.

10 No child—repeat: no child—is coming between you and sleeping 'til noon.

The Talk: Coming Out to Your Family

Not having babies is obviously something you've thought long and hard about, but keep in mind that your parents may be banking on one day having a wallet full of grandkids' pictures to show off to all their pals at the rest home. Carefully planned communication will make the news go down far easier.

Step One: Lay the Foundation

Nobody likes to be shocked. In the months and weeks leading up to The Talk, express ambivalence about having kids. Sigh loudly and say, "It's the funniest thing. I don't seem to have any nurturing instincts whatsoever." Introduce your puppy to your parents as their "new grandchild." If asked whether you've given any thought to having kids, abruptly stare off into space as though you've heard nothing, nothing at all.

Step Two: Set the Scene

When you're finally ready to announce your intentions, butter them up with dinner at a fancy restaurant. The public setting reduces the chances of mom or dad making a scene. The more froufrou the place, the less likely that a gurgling infant in an adjacent booth will add insult to injury. Be sure to clear the site of sharp objects in advance in case your mom suddenly flies into an ape-like rage.

Step Three: Accentuate the Positive

Don't say, "I'm sorry to inform you . . ." Slip into your newly acquired childfree persona, be it political abstainer or career champ, and then say something to the effect of, "Mom, dad, I have some great news! I've given it a lot of thought and have realized that the pitter-patter of little feet is not a sound I personally need to hear. Instead of having babies I'm moving to the Bahamas to become an artist and save the monkeys. Isn't that awesome?" Don't forget to mention the added benefits they will enjoy, like more freedom to travel and fewer holiday gifts to buy.

Step Four: Hold Your Ground

Your family may insist that you'll change your mind. They may pressure you to have kids for months and even years after you've shared the big news. Don't blow your top! Restate your intentions. For example, when mom wistfully says, "Gee, it sure would be nice to have some grandkids to spoil," you might reply, "Have you considered adopting a Hungarian orphan instead? I hear they're very cute, and house-broken." Or say, "Sure, no problem. I'll just go get knocked up tomorrow. You don't mind raising the thing, do you?" If you have siblings, be sure to pressure them to start their family sooner than later, which will take the heat off of you.

Step Five: Reward

Remind mom and dad often that they're still special, even without a wallet full of grandkid photos. "World's Best" mom and dad mugs, frames, cards, and T-shirts are a good start. Send them school-style pictures of your pets, and take them and the "kids" out to brunch on Grandparents Day so they don't feel left out. If you're able, use some of the extra disposable income you've accumulated thanks to not having kids to send them on that geezer cruise they've been longing for. Remind them frequently that they have you to enjoy without anyone else to get in the way. What could be better than that?

Reality Check! Getting unwanted attention for your childfree existence is unavoidable. Being childfree puts you in the minority, which in turn makes you stand out in a crowd. People with more curiosity than manners are going to ask annoying questions such as, "Do you mean no kids now or no kids ever?" and say dumb things like, "Yeah, I never wanted kids, but then one day I just blindly took the leap." Sadly, you can't stop people from being nosy, but you can shut them up with a quick, confident comeback. (See pages 22 and 136 for some handy replies.)

Spin-Cycle

It's not just your family that will need convincing. In some cases, friends with kids will try to cajole you into joining their tribe. When this happens, don't argue. Spin! It may take a while before the world catches on to the unsung pleasures of childfree living, but replacing phrases that represent outdated views with modern ones will ultimately help change minds!

When they call you . . .	You say . . .
Childless	Childfree
Cursed	Choosy
Barren	Walking bare-ass naked around the house whenever I please
Selfish	Selfless
Alone	In good company

When they say . . .	You reply . . .
You'll change your mind.	At least I can change my mind.
My kids are the best thing that ever happened to me.	My happiness isn't dependent on someone else.
There's never a right time to start having kids.	There's never a right time to start having kids.
It's the hardest job you'll ever do, and the most rewarding.	It's the hardest job you'll ever do for no money or appreciation.
Being a parent makes you a better person.	So does giving all your possessions to the poor, but that doesn't mean you do it.

Catching a Nonbreeder

You don't have to be coupled to be a confirmed non-breeder. If you're single and searching, you're going to have to filter out a lot of family-minded suitors to find that ideal person. Frequenting nonbreeding habitats and keeping your senses on alert for telltale mating calls and behaviors will make it easier to find that special someone, not someones.

Distinctive Mating Calls:

- Dating classified ad reads: "No kids. Not now. Not ever. I mean it, dammit!"

- Upon seeing a minivan, immediately yells, "Loser!"

- Card-carrying membership to a zero-population-growth organization

- Instinctively shudders whenever passing a park or school

- Wistfully says, "If only I'd been born infertile!"

Popular Nonbreeding Habitats:

- Apartment complex with signs that say, "Children found on the premises will be prosecuted."

- Bars and cafes, Sundays–Thursdays between 7 PM and 2 AM

- Monthly meetings of the local non-breeders club

- Bad school districts

- Your office, any time after 5 PM

- The outpatient waiting room at a tube-tying clinic

Common Mating Behaviors:

- Insists on using a condom, the pill, and spermicide

- Repeatedly refers to a pet as "the only child I can handle"

- Exhibits overdeveloped tastes in decorating and fashion

- Pursues a fulfilling career or hobbies (i.e., less likely to want to "fill the void")

- Will only meet you in childfree environments like bars, fancy restaurants, and strip clubs

Avoid at All Cost Dates Who:

- Make goo-goo eyes at the baby in the restaurant booth next to yours.

- Have a bassinet stashed in the spare closet "just in case."

- Talk wistfully about moving to the 'burbs someday.

- Honk and wave at school buses.

- Use phrases like "family-minded" in personal ads.

- Can think of nothing more fun to do on a Friday night than babysit.

Quick Replies for on the Fly

Why you don't want to have babies in fifteen words or less.
When the inevitable question arises, you will be ready.

Question
Why don't you have any children?

Answer
Earnest: Because I don't want any!

Witty: Why don't you have any manners?

End of conversation: I'm infertile, you jerk! (Burst out crying.)

Question
Are there any children on your horizon?

Answer
Earnest: Not the last time I looked.

Witty: No, but I think I spot a flock of geese.

End of conversation: Not since losing my reproductive organs in a gruesome fly-fishing accident.

Question
Soooooo, when do you think you'll be having kids?

Answer
Earnest: I have thought about it and have decided against it.

Witty: How about never? Is never good?

End of conversation: When minivans are sexy and day care is free.

Question
Aren't you getting to the age when you should be thinking about kids?

Answer
Earnest: Gosh, I really don't think that's anybody's business.

Witty: No, but you're getting to the age when you should know better than to ask.

End of conversation: Actually, I'm getting to the age when my ovaries start producing half-wits.

Babies on the horizon? Run for your lives!

Ten Conversations You Won't Have to Have

Telling people you're not having babies is hard, but think of all you'll never have to say.

1. "Sweetie, we have bad news about the tooth fairy."

2. "There's a reason your hamster hasn't moved in five days and smells like a fart."

3. "When a mommy loves a daddy and they share a bed and this stork appears and . . ."

4. "Did we make a big doodie today? Yes we did!"

5. "No, I haven't had the pleasure of viewing your scab collection."

6. "Garbage really isn't something we should put in our mouths."

7. "Honey pie, that man you call Santa Claus? Well, he's had a tad too much eggnog and he won't be coming around this year."

8. "Please don't stick your finger in there."

9. "I thought I made it crystal clear that we go pee-pee *before* getting into the car!"

10. "If you don't stop this very instant, we are turning around and there will be no cake for you. Is that understood?"

Subtle Reinforcements

Let's face it: It's a kid-centered world and people will naturally assume that you'll change your mind. These gentle and not-so-gentle reminders of your childfree status will make it clear over time that when you say no babies you mean no babies!

While holding someone else's baby, coo to it in your most cutesy baby voice, "Auntie Susie is never having babies, is she, wittle one? Noooo, dat would suck balls, wouldn't it my little poopsie woopsie? Auntie doesn't like the wittle babies, does she? Oogie oogie woo woo!"

Slap a "Baby Not on Board" bumper sticker on your two-seater sports car.

Every now and then, tell your friends, "You know, I may want kids after all." Pause a couple beats, then burst out, "Psych!"

Build a household shrine to Planned Parenthood founder Margaret Sanger or a childfree role model (see page 26 for a list). Frame the great dame's picture and set it on the mantle above your fireplace. Surround it with candles, incense, flowers, and offerings of candy and other trinkets.

Have your doctor or vet do an ultrasound of your or your significant other's fetus-free uterus. Place the printout on the fridge and point to it proudly whenever people are over.

Refer to your pets as "my kids" and complain frequently about how needy and jealous they are.

Every year or so, make plans (jet off to Cannes for a decadent month of wine and cinema, enroll in graduate school, accept a promotion with longer hours) and/or purchases (two-seater car, a fixer-upper cabin in the woods) that clearly preclude any chances of having children.

Role Models

Being an unparent in a world that's ga-ga for the family lifestyle can be very lonely at times. But rest assured you are in good company. These are just a few modern childfree successes whose examples you can look to for inspiration.

JULIA CHILD, celebrity chef, never "ate for two."

KATHARINE HEPBURN, actress, never turned down a role because she was too tied up with little ones.

ROBERT SMITH, lead singer of The Cure, is a proud and extremely cool uncle.

BILL BLASS, fashion designer, would rather die than have baby barf stain his fabulous lapels.

MOTHER TERESA, saint, had her hands full with the world's least-wanted children.

DOLLY PARTON, country singer, knows well that 9 to 5 is more than enough time to spend working each day.

OPRAH, media goddess, put ratings before rugrats and says she's never regretted it.

HELEN CLARK, New Zealand prime minister, took political heat for remaining childfree, but how else would she have time to run "Middle Earth"?

THEODOR SEUSS GEISEL, as in *children's* book author/genius Dr. Seuss, clearly had his hands full with his inner child.

GEORGIA O'KEEFFE, artist, created G-rated flowers with X-rated overtones.

ALLEN GINSBERG, Beat poet, liked his boys young, but not that young.

BO DEREK, actress, proves you don't have to be a mama to be one hot mama.

TERRY GROSS, National Public Radio interviewer, decided to tune into her highly respected radio show rather than some little one's squeals.

STEVIE NICKS, rock star, took her romance with band mates on the road, but left her maternal instincts at home.

JANET RENO, former U.S. Attorney General, felt it was enough to lay down the law for an entire country; imagine if she'd had to do it at home, too.

J. EDGAR HOOVER, infamous F.B.I. director, couldn't decide whether he wanted to be the mommy or the daddy.

ANGELA BASSET, actress, never had to get her groove back because she never lost it.

RALPH NADER, consumer activist, saved so many children with all the car safety and seat-belt laws he got passed that he never needed any of his own.

EUDORA WELTY, novelist, didn't win that O. Henry Award (or the Medal for Literature, or the American Book Award, or the Pulitzer Prize) for making critically acclaimed babies.

WALT WHITMAN, poet, produced only high-voltage poetry with his body electric.

AYN RAND, novelist and philosopher, had only her own potential to realize.

DOROTHY PARKER, poet, was better at drinking and suffering than procreating.

CHRISTOPHER WALKEN, actor, scares children.

Why should pregnant women have all the fun?

Celebrate!

If subtle reinforcements aren't enough, nothing cements your membership in the childfree camp better than throwing yourself an unbaby shower! Incorporate some of these ideas into your bash to make it a huge success.

INVITES: Send them out on traditional baby shower invitation stationery, but write in "un" before "baby shower" and stamp a big "X" over the traditional bassinet or stork motif. Word it to the effect of, "You are cordially invited to celebrate my exciting child-free future!" Be sure to include a line that asks parents to leave their little ones at home.

GIFT REGISTRY: When a friend has a baby, everyone is expected to cough up a present. Why should they get to enjoy all the booty? If you want to treat your inner child, register at your favorite toy store. You may also go naughty and request lingerie. Child-unfriendly knives, china, or stemware also make a fine choice. Or, in lieu of gifts request that guests donate money to the population-control organization of your choice.

DÉCOR: Banners! Streamers! Spare no expense! Set out a frame that says "baby" but leave it empty or insert your own picture. Have your favorite pair of shoes cast in pewter. Hang deflated balloons to symbolize empty wombs. Put the TV on mute and play movies that feature evil children (see page 48 for a list). Set out discarded birth control compacts filled with confetti.

DRINKS: Pink Cosmos for the girl you'll never have and Blue Curaçao cocktails (try 3 parts lime vodka, 1 part blue curaçao, with a splash of Sprite/7Up) for the boy. Buy a bunch of those teeny-weenie plastic babies and skewer them with toothpicks to use as drink garnishes. Serve in baby bottles if you want to be super saucy.

FOOD: Think grown-up food, the stuff no child ever touches: caviar, smoked salmon, stuffed mushrooms, pungent cheeses, carpaccio, finger sandwiches with crust, anchovies, tofu, and vegetables galore—including broccoli, Brussels sprouts, spinach, and asparagus.

GAMES: Thank your lucky stars and the effectiveness of modern-day birth control techniques: there will be no juvenile eating-chocolate-ice-cream-out-of-a-diaper or pinning-a-diaper-to-a-baby-doll-while-blindfolded games at your adult gathering. Instead, have friends guess the circumference of your unspoiled waistline. Get a stork piñata and beat it to a sugary pulp; it won't come a knockin' on your door after that display of unchecked id. Play "pin the screaming child on the harried soccer mom." Tape descriptions of childfree celebrities on people's backs; the first person to guess them all wins.

GRAB BAGS: Don't forget to send everyone home with a few condoms to ensure that all the other nonbreeders in attendance stay that way!

Life is good at 0 decibels.

Sharp Edges

Welcome to your childfree lifestyle!

NOT HAVING KIDS isn't just a choice you've made; it's a fabulous lifestyle as well! Your career, your home, your clothing, your diet, your physical health, your friendships, and even your tastes in entertainment will be greatly affected by your lack of off-spring, nearly always for the better.

YOU'LL NEVER HAVE to turn down a great career opportunity because it conflicts with family, though you may decide to take a few years off to "find yourself" in the Himalayas. Nor will you have to compromise your well-honed taste in fashion or décor to make room for child-friendly shapes and stain-resistant fabrics and primary colors. Whether your dream is to become a rock star or the first amateur wrestler to pilot a rocket into space, your personal development will continue unimpeded until you reach a ripe old age.

OF COURSE, society as a whole is still geared to meet the needs of families. Living it up in a world overcrowded with minivans, miniature golf courses, and mini malls can be a challenge at times, but not one that can't be overcome with a little ingenuity. Making the most of what you have—which is quite a lot, by the way—is what the childfree lifestyle is all about!

A Saturday in the Life

You may be blissfully unaware of it, but your decision not to have kids affects your day from the first hints of sunrise until long after the stars come out.

You

Noon Oooh. Tough call. Should you have the pomegranate mimosa or the classic Bloody Mary?

10am Mmmmmmm, pillow soft.

2pm *Namaste,* baby!

11am Rested and ready to face the day!

4pm Nap time. Gotta rest up for your big night out.

1pm You can just squeeze in a much-needed facial before yoga practice!

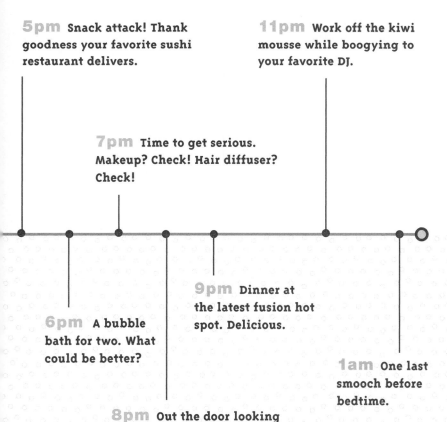

5pm Snack attack! Thank goodness your favorite sushi restaurant delivers.

11pm Work off the kiwi mousse while boogying to your favorite DJ.

7pm Time to get serious. Makeup? Check! Hair diffuser? Check!

9pm Dinner at the latest fusion hot spot. Delicious.

6pm A bubble bath for two. What could be better?

1am One last smooch before bedtime.

8pm Out the door looking like a million bucks.

You with Kids

6am Wake to the sounds of cartoon violence blaring from the living room TV.

11am Out of mini corndogs again? Everyone to the minivan. It's time for a Costco run!!!

8am Have a talk with the kids about not putting Silly Putty in your coffee.

9am How many onesies can a baby go through in one week? You lose count at 38 while loading the washing machine.

7am Junior just barfed half-digested cereal onto the trampoline. Have fun cleaning that mesh!

1pm Your exercise for the day: Breaking up a fight between two super-aggro soccer dads.

8pm Read the bedtime story about the aardvark and the llama yet again.

2pm Attend a cartoon matinee with 500 other squirmy kids and their long-suffering parents.

5pm Eat pizza while being serenaded by gigantic off-key puppets.

10pm Zzzzzzzzzzzzzzzzz.

4pm Shop for somebody else's shoes.

9pm Can you keep awake long enough to pump some extra breast milk for the week ahead?

7pm Call in vain for a babysitter who's actually available next Friday night.

| BABY **NOT** ON BOARD

Most people don't know how great it is
until they've lost it forever.

Pamper Isn't a Diaper

Maybe parents deserve a break, but by not having kids, you're the one who can afford to take one.

With the money you save on . . .	You could . . .
A month's worth of pureed carrots	Get a manicure/pedicure
A month's worth of diapers	Treat yourself to a massage
A fancy new stroller	Go on a weekend getaway
Monthly childcare	Afford the mortgage on a nicer home
18 years of birthday parties	Take a luxury cruise with your partner of choice
A minivan	Drive a convertible with all the trimmings

Reality Check! In spite of numerous technological and medical advances, women get the short end of the stick when it comes to having a baby. It's the gal who has to carry a backbreaking watermelon in her belly for nine months, during three of which the mother-to-be barfs frequently and suffers from constant exhaustion, followed by the really fun hip separation, which causes her to walk like a mortally wounded penguin. After that, some-one's still got to get the damned thing out of the poor lady whether by forceps or incision or sheer determination. And men? All they have to do is smoke a cigar and make a home movie that nobody, but nobody, wants to see.

Man: Vive la Différence!

Although some people say there's nothing more attractive than a guy with kids, some people are wrong (for more on this, see Reality Check! on page 76). Chiseled masculine lines have a way of softening when kids come into the picture. Style tends to take a backseat to practicality. And that refreshing, fun outlook? Bid it farewell as worry and responsibility take over.

You	You with Kids
Wear shades inside and outside	There's no hiding those worry lines.
Tattoo in plain sight	Icky scarring from where tattoo was lasered off
Paperback in pocket shows your mind is still engaged	List of chores in pocket indicates you're behind
Welcoming stance says, "Ready for good times!"	Aggressive stance says, "I mean business!"
Styled haircut demonstrates you're still in the game	No-frills haircut shows convenience is preferred over style
Disposable income burning hole in pocket	Wallet empty after paying preschool tuition this month
Undeniably fashionable and up-to-date duds	Rumpled clothes that pre-date junior's birth
Perfect posture thanks to regular workouts and massages	Slumped shoulders! Playing horsey sure does take its toll.
Since when is it OK to ever be seen without a martini?	Since when is it considered sexy for a man to carry a diaper bag?

Woman: Your Body, All to Yourself

'Tis the frustrating fate of all women to suffer from body issues of one kind or another, and don't even get started with the pressures of keeping up with ever-changing fashion trends. But ladies who don't opt for the family lifestyle at least have the consolation that it could be worse, way worse.

Your Feminine Body Issues

Long hair takes a lot of work, but at least you don't have to worry about some kid yanking it out all the time.

Faint bags under your eyes from partying too hard, but your designer eyewear hides them well.

Sore, swollen boobs from PMSing. (Hooray! You're not pregnant!)

Headache resulting from one too many amaretto sours last night, you bad thing, you.

Shopping 'til you drop sure does take its toll on your shoulders.

Achy back from a hard-core trainer-supervised workout.

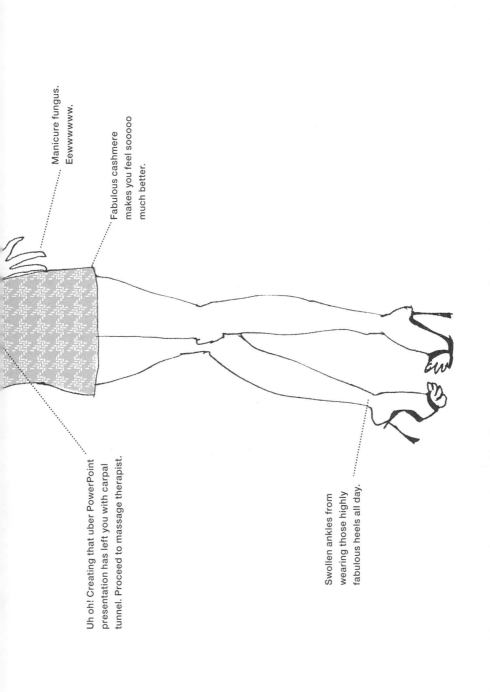

Your Feminine Body Issues with Kids

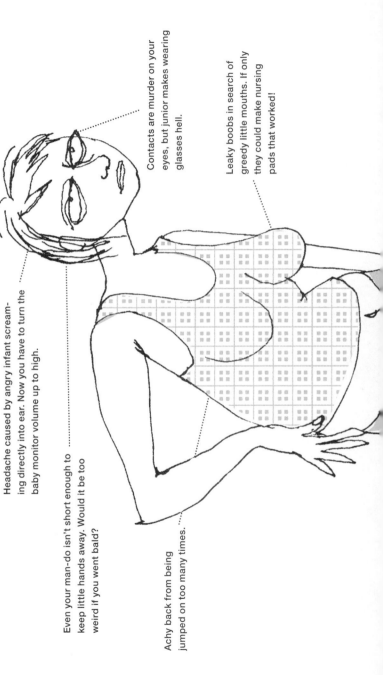

Headache caused by angry infant screaming directly into ear. Now you have to turn the
baby monitor volume up to high.

Even your man-do isn't short enough to
keep little hands away. Would it be too
weird if you went bald?

Achy back from being
jumped on too many times.

Contacts are murder on your
eyes, but junior makes wearing
glasses hell.

Leaky boobs in search of
greedy little mouths. If only
they could make nursing
pads that worked!

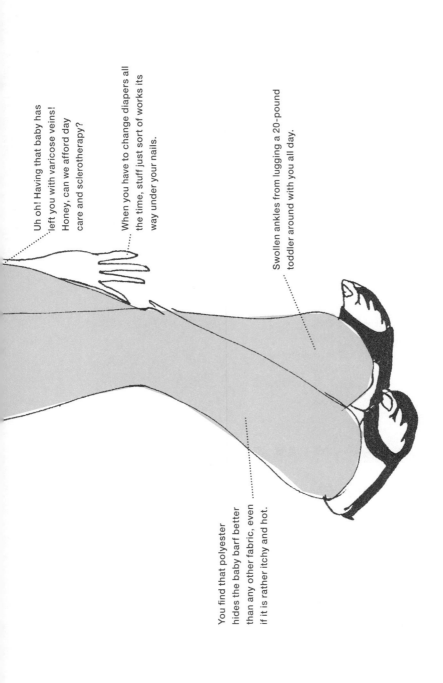

Uh oh! Having that baby has left you with varicose veins! Honey, can we afford day care and sclerotherapy?

When you have to change diapers all the time, stuff just sort of works its way under your nails.

Swollen ankles from lugging a 20-pound toddler around with you all day.

You find that polyester hides the baby barf better than any other fabric, even if it is rather itchy and hot.

Make Money, Not Babies

Disposable income? Here's how you spend it and how you could be spending it if you had kids.

Your Disposable Income	Your Disposable Income with Kids
25% entertainment (film festivals, theater season passes, sporting events)	25% entertainment (cartoon matinees, puppets on ice, *The Nutcracker*)
20% lessons (skydiving, sushi-making, tantric yoga . . .)	20% lessons (piano, ballet, soccer, math . . .)
20% fusion restaurant dining	20% frozen pizzas and corn dogs
15% froufrou drinks	15% baby formula
10% monthly facials, waxes, and peels	10% family therapy
10% shoes	10% diaper service

Mi Casa Es Mi Casa!

Childfree decorating is all about making a statement: My home is mine, all mine! Of course there are many elegant approaches you can take that would be impossible to pull off if you had kids, including these popular ones.

ETERNAL FRAT: Never learned to clean up after yourself? Lava lamp hasn't been turned off since 1984? Congratulations! No need to go changing now.

CHIC FREAK: Unlike the Jetsons, you don't have to worry about that nuisance Elroy jumping on your beloved Herman Miller chair.

ANTIQUES SHOW HO: Alabaster is your middle name, and owning the oldest and finest is your game.

ZEN MINIMALIST: The living room is a blank palate, a place to liberate your mind. So is the bathroom, the bedroom, the office, the sauna. And that ain't no "sandbox" in your backyard neither.

POST-MARTHA MANIAC: Martha may have done hard time for her white-collar crime, but that doesn't mean you can't continue her legacy of perfect, perfect, and more perfect.

MAD SCIENTIST: Hey, you've got plans for that bacteria growing in the back of your fridge. And hands off the mold garden in the bathroom.

Not-So-Empty Nest

Got a spare room that isn't filled with the pitter-pat of little feet? Don't let that space go to waste! Here are some ideas for how to turn that "empty nest" into a rockin' roost.

RUMPUS ROOM: Keep your inner child entertained with all the latest audio-visual toys.

CRAFT ROOM: Create, don't procreate! And feel free to run with those scissors while you're at it.

HOME OFFICE: Think how productive you'll be with nobody interrupting you.

GYM: Your body is home to the only DNA you have. Treat it well!

WET BAR: Serve up your famously potent cocktails with a roomful of class!

DUNGEON: Not everyone is as kinky as you. Then again, not everyone has their own cage complete with leather cuffs and feather duster.

MEDITATION CENTER: Bliss out on the peace and quiet that comes with an empty nest!

GUEST ROOM: Be an extra-gracious host or hostess and give out-of-towners a place to bed down that isn't a pull-out sofa.

NURSERY: For prize-winning orchids, that is.

The Quintessential Kid-Unfriendly Movie Library

A child-inappropriate movie library is the staple of any warm, caring, childfree household. Here are a few titles no adult haven should be without!

Rosemary's Baby
Strung-out skinny woman makes devil spawn and learns to love it!

Children of the Corn
Jebediah Junior's gone and chopped up the pretty lady!

The Bad Seed
The parents aren't to blame for this pint-sized princess's appetite for murder. Or are they?

The Stepford Wives
First you have kids. Then you move to the suburbs. Next thing you know, you've been replaced by a robot who simply adores cooking and folding socks. Consider yourself warned!

The Exorcist
Just an average kid suffering the throes of puberty, or demon-possessed maniac with a thing for bloody cruci-fixes? Either way, it's pretty ugly.

Willy Wonka & the Chocolate Factory
The lesson here? Not all kids are bad, but most are greedy, lying, sniveling little meanies who, in this movie, get what they deserve.

Larry Clark's Kids
So long, mom. I'm off to spread fatal sexually transmitted diseases! Don't wait up for me!

Mommie Dearest
It's not that Joan Crawford doesn't deserve a bad rap, but who wouldn't be driven mad by having kids?

Village of the Damned
They're well-dressed, well-behaved, extremely intelligent, and self-entertaining. Except for the high body count and the whole evil spawn from outer space thing, these kids are perfect!

The Omen

Hooray! We have a son! Oh no! He's the antichrist! Will Gregory Peck have what it takes to take little Damian out with the seven daggers of Meggado?

The Innocents

Being a governess isn't so bad, unless your charges are being manipulated by vile forces from beyond the grave.

The Brood

Stressed-out woman goes into deep psychotherapy only to manifest a pack of deformed children eager to get blood on their hands.

The Good Son

It's kid vs. kid in this tale of boyhood friendship gone sick and wrong, featuring a devilish *Home Alone* star Macaulay Culkin and an angelic Elijah Wood (a.k.a. Frodo).

It's Alive

When the baby gets scared, the baby kills in this gory B-movie on the dark side of starting a family.

Child's Play

The kid's alright, but not his doll, who happens to be possessed with the vengeful ghost of a serial killer.

A.I.

When fertility treatments aren't working, consider adopting a creepy robot child with a serious oedipal complex.

The Shining

Discipline takes a dark turn in this spooky film based on Stephen King's novel about a father pushed to his limits. The child's repeated screaming of "red rum" would make anyone want to reach for the nearest ax.

No Barriers

Just imagining what would happen to your home-sweet-home if you had kids is enough to make you want to get your tubes tied and your hardwood floors refinished!

Your Home

Your Home with Kids

Sick Days to Spare

You'd think the decision not to have kids wouldn't have any bearing on work. After all, work is work, family is family, never the twain shall meet. Right? Wrong! Whether or not you publicize your intentions to remain childfree, your lack of kids will undoubtedly have an impact on your life at the office.

Pros	Cons
With your workday focus uninterrupted by family stress, you'll get promotions faster and enjoy more money than your baby-making co-workers.	Your promotion and raise were earned partly for picking up the slack during an onslaught of family leaves.
There's nobody to interrupt you during that stressful presentation.	There's nobody to interrupt you during that stressful presentation.
When you wake up in the morning, the only person you have to motivate is yourself.	When it comes to making excuses for lateness, your nasty hangover doesn't compare to little Bobbie's botulism.
Without a gazillion annoying baby pictures to clutter your office, your workspace qualifies as downright tasteful.	You're subjected to a gazillion photographs of other people's little munchkins en route to your baby photo–free desk.

Pros	Cons
Who can attend that conference in Fiji? You can attend that conference in Fiji! Don't forget the suntan oil!	Nobody sympathizes with your struggles to find a decent dog-sitter while you're away at that conference in Fiji.
With the money you save on child care alone, you can afford the nicest suit, the sexiest car, and the plastic surgery that will keep you looking like the great success that you are.	Not being a member of the parent club means you'll be treated like an outsider and may get the ugly end of office politics now and then.
You'll never bore anybody with stories of how your little pookie wookie is the smartest, cutest thing in sneakers.	Your co-workers still think you'll be interested in hearing about how Craigie Junior took three whole steps yesterday.
Saving for retirement is a breeze with no college tuition to pay; and with no grandchildren to stick around for, you can do whatever you like.	You won't be able to park your RV for free at your grandkid's house during your umpteenth cross-country drive.

Speed	0 to 60 whenever you please
Handling	Takes corners like a NASCAR race car
Body	Two doors and no need for more
Interior	Leather, sweet leather
Exterior	Pop the top and experience the open road the way the good Lord intended.
Safety	Safe enough for you to have fun and look good
Storage	Room for a picnic basket in the trunk
Features	Who needs cup-holders? You have time to drink your coffee.
Audio/Visual	NC-17 lyrics, jazz, classic hits from your youth

Your Car with Kids

Speed	0 to 60 in about 18 years
Handling	1-mile turn radius
Body	More secret doors than a game show
Interior	Mystery crumbs in the upholstery
Exterior	Add a few paper flowers and you've got a parade-worthy float.
Safety	Airbags everywhere, for the padded-room effect.
Storage	How many toys can you fit into one backseat?
Features	99 cup-holders, filled to capacity with sticky residue
Audio/Visual	The TV monitor lets you listen to cartoons instead of whining.

Your Dinner

Your Dinner with Kids

Eggs & Dairy
Fondue
Lattes
Crème caramel
Artisinal cheeses

Fruits & Veggies
Edible undies
Chardonnay
Steamed white asparagus
Brandied baked pears

Meat, Fish & Poultry
Lobster bisque
Kobe beef
Foie gras
Roasted quail

Carbohydrates
Sushi, sushi, sushi
French toast
Beer bread
Rum cake

Your Diet

Eggs & Dairy
Strawberry-flavored milk
Frozen pizza
Twinkie pie
Green eggs and ham

Fruits & Veggies
Juice boxes
Individually sliced grapes
Jell-O
Pureed carrots

Meat, Fish & Poultry
Tuna casserole
Processed meat product
Corn dogs
Beef chili

Carbohydrates
Boxed macaroni and cheese
Animal-shaped crackers
Graham crackers
Toaster tarts

Your Diet with Kids

Spoil Your Inner Child Rotten

Some things are just too good to throw away on kids.

Jell-O (as in Jell-O shots)

Themed birthday parties

Comic books

Piñatas (filled with mini-bottles of booze)

Education

Video games

Ice cream

Glow sticks

Halloween

Confetti

Happy Meals

Bubble baths

Cartoons

Pee-Wee Herman

Parks

Curiosity

Harry Potter books

Sea-Monkeys

Shel Silverstein

Recess

Play dates

Learning about nature

Cloud watching

Snow angels

Fun bandages

Superhero underwear

Board games

Prime numbers

Saturday mornings

The shallow end

Made-up words

A sense of wonder

Puppy eyes

Movie-star crushes

Dance/music/martial arts classes

Cupcakes

Nose picking

Kazoos

Playing hooky

Twister

Slumber parties

Forts

Cool sneakers

Lunch boxes

Ponytails

Cuddly stuffed animals

High metabolism

Talent shows

Imaginary friends

Hot chocolate

Discounts

Chewable vitamins

Forget About It

Parents are forced to relive some of the lowest moments of their own lives through their children. But pat yourself on the back, because you'll never have to go through these again.

Algebra

State reports

Playground bullies

Reciting the preamble to the Constitution

School "lunch"

$e=mc^2$

Memorizing the layers of the earth's crust

Being picked last for dodgeball

If Train A is heading 20 miles per hour in X direction . . .

Teen acne

The prom

College-entrance exams

Puppy love

First breakup

The five-paragraph essay

Virginity

Spelling bees

First hangover

Ritalin withdrawl

Like dogs, children can smell your fear.

Other People's Children

Keeping your cool in a world filled with drool

THEY ARE CALLED Other People's Children, and there is no escaping them! Some OPCs are cute and cuddly. Others are quiet and polite. A few, however, are demented, squalling troublemakers who will stop at nothing until they've destroyed something, anything, be it your silence, your prized end table, your hairdo, or your lucky martini glass. And like it or not, at some point in your life you're going to have to deal with all of them.

FORTUNATELY FOR YOU, numerous tried-and-true tactics exist for making the most of your life among OPCs—whether you're nice enough to babysit your charming niece or never want to be asked to change a diaper again. The first step is to get a basic understanding of the average OPC. Being able to tell the mouth from the bum is crucial; knowing the vaccination schedule is not. From there you'll need to separate the good OPCs from the bad, that is, those for whom there's room in your life and those who fall under your zero-tolerance policy. Sure, interacting with youngsters isn't always easy, but with just a little knowledge and a can-do attitude, dealing with the OPCs that do come your way can be rewarding, interesting, and occasionally even fun.

OPCs: A Developmental Chart

Chances are you've never really felt the need to learn about children. True, it doesn't require a degree for someone to have an OPC, but for you to handle one correctly—that is, to your advantage—does require a bit of knowledge and skill. Whether the OPC in question is a squirmy baby or a gangly teen, everything you need to know is summarized below for easy reference.

Baby

HEAD—Head is soft and squishy. Try not to bang it against anything.

MOUTH—Slobber central! Also baby's primary means of exploring the world. Keep well-sealed with pacifier, bottle, or other non-choking-hazard object.

NECK—Rubbery, especially just after birth. Works best propped up against a hand, knee, or bouncy chair.

BELLY BUTTON—Once an umbilical cord, now a site of great pleasure. Place mouth directly on top of it and go *thrrrrrpppttttt* to illicit happy smiles and giggles.

BOTTOM—Do not be fooled by the deceptive cuteness of this soft, doughy pillow. It emits yellow and green stinky ooze at regular intervals. Keep under tight wrap!

LEGS—Baby fat! No need to panic and buy junior a gym membership. Unsightly pudge on a baby is actually considered a good thing, some even find it cute, weirdly enough.

TOES—"Piggies," in baby parlance. As in, "This little piggy went to market. This little piggy stayed home . . ."

Toddler

HEAD—Headstrong is more like it. Toddlers are characterized by their refusal to comply with reasonable requests.

MOUTH—Noisemaker central! Elicits screams and defiant "No's" when

LEGS—Nearly always in motion, these propel toddler forward at rapid, dangerous speeds.

FEET—Seem to grow at an unnaturally fast clip. Require frequent reshoeing.

School-aged Child

HEAD—Expensive to maintain between braces, glasses, and carnival face paint.

toddler does not get his way. Protect yourself with earplugs or headphones.

NOSE—Bacteria-infested snot faucet. Wash hands immediately if they come into contact.

NECK—Resist the urge to strangle.

HANDS—When left idle, these can cause serious damage thanks to refined motor control. Keep occupied with fuzzy objects.

PRIVATES—Frequently mistaken by toddler for squeeze toys. Avert your eyes.

BOTTOM—Wet and solid waste are now distinguishable from one another, but child requires extensive potty training to gain control of these functions.

MOUTH—Capable of creating complete sentences and engaging in actual conversations, though usually on meaningless topics.

SHOULDERS—Able to carry heavy loads via backpack. Load 'er up!

HANDS—Capable of besting any adult when holding a joystick connected to the latest video game. Competing is futile.

BOTTOM—The topic of much potty humor, which the school-aged child finds endlessly amusing.

LEGS & FEET—Useful for running, ballet practice, sports, and any other activity that will eventually exhaust the child.

Teenager

HEAD—One of the largest oil-producers in the world. Resist the temptation to gawk.

MOUTH—Grows temporarily foul as teen learns to make use of four-letter words and slang.

EARS—Temporary deafness leads many teens to listen to tuneless pop music at eardrum-shattering volumes.

NECK & SHOULDERS—Exhibit a tendency to slouch unappealingly, especially in the presence of adults.

BELLY—As flat, slender, and hairless as it will ever be in the OPCs lifetime. Sigh.

PRIVATES—Just itching to get out and produce more OPCs. Keep well stocked

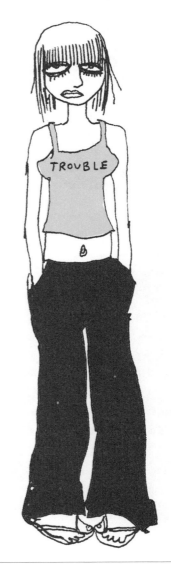

with condoms and other protective supplies.

LEGS—Too big for their britches, that's for sure!

FEET—Begin emitting a strange, salty odor. Should remain covered at all times.

College Student

HEAD—Giddy with uninformed ideals, useless knowledge, and sexual fantasies. Feel free to add your own thoughts and perspective to this spongelike entity.

MOUTH—A.k.a. beer funnel. Also a popular repository for Jagermeister shots and pizza.

EARS—In more evolved college students, actually capable of listening to what you say.

HIPS & BELLY—Site of the dreaded "Freshman 15" weight gain. (*See* mouth.)

PRIVATES—Site of OPC's first case of VD.

SHOULDERS—Finally strong enough to help with serious chores. Put these puppies to work constructing your wet bar!

LEGS & FEET—Able to carry this OPC into the real world and the realm of adults.

Little Devils

Kids are taught never to talk to strange adults. Well, the same advice applies to unparents when it comes to kids. Sure the pint-sized flirt in the supermarket check-out line may seem sweet as vanilla-flavored vodka, but she could also start screaming at any second, which is not something you need in your life. For some kids, alas, ignoring them is not enough. When confronted by a little monster, even the most understanding of unparents may start to lose his cool. Use these strategies to cope with the occasional brat out of hell.

Airplane Kickers

When you're at 30,000 feet, there's no escaping these little rascals. Ask your friendly flight attendant to let you switch seats and make your flight a bit less turbulent. If you can afford it, fly business class or at least take the red-eye. Avoid flying on weekends and to popular family destinations.

Supermarket Screamers

You'd like to take the sugar cereal they're demanding and pour it down their little throats. Alas, you can't. You can keep a walkman on hand to tune these loud-speakers out. Better yet, head to the chichi organic grocer instead and linger in the bitter greens section for as long as possible. Shop-ping late at night will also reduce your run-ins with these high-pitch OPCs.

Movie Wreckers

If shushing fails, be a hero. Head to the lobby and get a manager to throw the baby and its rude parents out! While it's no guarantee, attending later showings, art-house cinemas, and kid-inappropriate films will lessen your chances of having one of these dramatic off-screen encounters.

Pint-Sized Neighbors of Doom

You don't just buy a home, you get the neighborhood and the neighbor's children as well. Nip their "boundary issues" in the bud by snarling every time you see them. If they walk by,

quickly draw the curtains. They'll get the message soon enough. If you'd rather not bother, consider moving to a neighborhood that's known to have poor schools (though this could backlash and land you in a nest of undereducated OPCs with mischief on their minds).

Tantrum Tommies/Theresas

It's unavoidable. You're innocently walking down the sidewalk or trying to maneuver your way to the gift shop when suddenly a horrible scene unfolds before you. A child stops mid-stride and begins to scream. Who cares what about? Oh, they will get their way. They will! They will! They will! They will! Best advice? Get out of their way. Cross the street. Run. Don't forget to scowl disapprovingly at the OPC as you hurry past.

Dining Disasters

Don't let these food-flingers destroy your dining experience! Dine on the late side so as to avoid the 6 PM family rush or become well-acquainted with pub grub. Steering clear of restaurants with themes, animal mascots, and video games in favor of fancier fare is also a good call. See page 70 for more tips on how to keep your dining experiences disaster-free.

Does This Restaurant Cater to Children?

You don't spend good money on dining out only to end up feeling like you're eating on the set of *Romper Room*. Be sure to check the menu carefully before selecting an eatery.

kids menu

Dinner served from 4 PM until 8 PM

APPETIZERS

Complimentary crayons

Booster seats

Paper napkins

SIDE DISHES

Cartoon mascot

Extra butter knife for cutting food into bite-sized chunks

Little League celebration happening in the adjacent room

Tater tots

MAIN COURSE

Hot dogs à la carte

Perky waitress who checks in on you every five seconds

Everything comes with fries

BEVERAGES

Free refills on sugary sodas

DESSERT

A rousing rendition of "Happy Birthday" sung by the staff

Ice-cream sundaes, our specialty

All meals are served in easy-to-wipe plastic booths. Don't forget to ask about our free extra-wide minivan parking!

Le Menu
Dinner served from 7 PM until midnight

....

Appetizers

Convenient downtown location

Chic, modern design

Spiffy dress code

Side Dishes

Celebrity sightings

Substantial tax write-off

Adjacent bar serves froufrou
drinks while you wait

Oysters, oysters, oysters

Main course

Wait staff so good looking you
want to gobble them up

Bib—for cracking shellfish,
of course

Exotic flavors and fusion delights
with unpronounceable names

Beverages

Wine list longer than the novel
you're reading

Dessert

Alcoholic flambé

Time to linger and savor
every bite

....

Enjoy a sophisticated meal in our invigorating, ambient atmosphere.
Valet parking available.

Fly Kids Free

Nothing spoils a vacation like a pool full of urinating, screaming vermin. Don't want a pack of unruly tykes to ruin your next getaway? While there's no avoiding children altogether, these guideposts will help direct you to places where families fear to tread.

UNHAPPY TRAILS

- The brochure boasts family-friendly accommodations!

- It's located within 100 miles of an amusement park.

- The hotel has a "theme."

- The hotel marquee reads "Welcome Junior Beauty Pageant Contestants!"

- The taxicabs are equipped with seat belts.

- There's a babysitter on the premises.

- The airlines offer "kids fly free" deals to the location.

- The brochure explicitly states that guests under the age of 18 aren't welcome.

- The Centers for Disease Control has issued a warning for this place.

- The swimming pool has a bar where the shallow end used to be.

- It requires a long flight and several terrifying boat rides to get there.

- A child visitor is likely to see something there that will be uncomfortable for parents to explain (i.e., brothel, war memorial, casino).

- Museums and opera are the main attractions.

- Only exotic, spicy foods are served.

Are You Cool Aunt/Uncle Material?

Of course, there may be youngsters in your life that you can't avoid—your newborn nephew, for example, or your best friend's newly adopted daughter. With these little ones, the unparent faces a tough choice: whether or not to play the role of Cool Aunt or Uncle. Being Cool certainly isn't for everyone. It takes the right combination of patience, discipline, and cunning to do the job well. If your childfree persona is Peter Pan, the task will be easy; if it's Sprog Snob, then you probably won't get far, which is fine as well. Take this quiz to figure out whether you're ready, in need of more practice, or shouldn't even bother.

1 *Your brother proudly presents his newborn child to you. It looks just like the worm you accidentally squished this morning. How do you respond?*

A) "Oh. I am so sorry. I hope it's not permanent."

B) "Awwww. Cute little bugger! Looks just like you!"

C) "That's nice. How long 'til it knows how to say my name?"

2 *Your young nephew Fabio is touching his willy—all the time. What's your response?*

A) Tell Fabio a scary story about the little boy who grew hair on his palms before going blind.

B) Ask his parents whether they are aware of Fabio's—ahem!—masturbation issues.

C) Wink and say, "Yeah, I have a go at it myself now and then."

3 *Your friend's daughter Susie is having a birthday party. Which is the most appropriate gift?*

A) Nothing. Suze is lucky you even showed up.

B) Art supplies. You want to encourage Susie's little mind.

C) The Barbie convertible that was deemed "too extravagant" by The Suzester's uptight parents.

4 *Where do you keep the pictures your friends send you of their progeny?*

A) Circular file. Where else?

B) On the fridge, until they fade and peel off.

C) In a frame that you set out whenever the kids are in the house and put away as soon as they're gone.

5 *In a rare act of extreme generosity, you've offered to babysit a good friend's 11-year-old son, Stanley. What's on the agenda?*

A) Set Stanley up with a stack of videos and a frozen dinner. You'll be in the next room if he needs anything.

B) A play date with another friend's child. Surely the two of them will find a way to entertain each other.

C) Pizza oink fest, followed by screenings of your all-time favorite '70s sci-fi horror flicks. When you scream, be sure it's for ICE CREAM!

6 *Tell the wittle pumpkins wumpkins a bedtime story:*

A) "There once was a scary green monster that ate children who didn't fall asleep this very second. The end."

B) "Once upon a time in a faraway place, lived a princess . . ."

C) "Have I ever told you about the time your cool auntie got put in jail and woke up with a big tattoo of an aardvark on her behind?"

7 *Your pal's toddler Lolly is coming over. How do you prepare?*

A) Thank goodness you've got an empty closet with a lock on it just waiting for an occupant. Lolly want a lockup?

B) You call the friend last minute and suggest meeting up elsewhere. You're just not up for little guests.

C) A box of cool toys left over from your childhood ought to keep Lolly occupied while you prep the martinis.

8 *Your brother's kid has just learned that Santa Claus is a fraud. He's devastated. What's the best way to comfort him?*

A) "Whatever, kid. You just wait until you touch your first fake boob. That's devastation."

B) Upset kids are devastating to you. You'll be avoiding your nephew until he chills out.

C) "Just between you and me, I think your parents are completely wrong about this whole Santa Claus thing. Seriously, I'm pretty sure I saw him last night at an art opening."

9 *You've just learned that a friend's kid got rejected from the preschool of her choice. What's your response?*

A) "Preschools have admissions now? Sucks for you."

B) Suggest that there are other perfectly good preschools in the world that would be happy to have her.

C) Who's up for doorbell ditching a certain preschool principal's house tonight?

10 *How do you think your nieces and nephews (current and/or future) will remember you?*

A) As the sour-faced meany who gave them prunes on Halloween.

B) That pleasant yet dull person who hovered around the cheese plate on holidays.

C) As their personal idol who they want to be just like when they grow up.

SCORING: Give yourself three points for every C answer, two points for every B answer, and one point for every A answer.

How cool are you?

23–30 POINTS: Welcome to the club, baby! You truly are too cool for school, which you undoubtedly encourage your nephew or niece to skip now and then in order to "suckle upon the rich marrow of life." Because your time with children is limited, you make the most of it, but are more than happy to hand the impressionable little tyke back at the end of the day.

16–22 POINTS: You, dear, are playing it cool. Sure you "love" your darling nephew or niece and you try your best to set a good example and be nice, but you aren't exactly going out of your way to cultivate a meaningful relationship or anything. There's no shame in your game, though you may want to spice things up now and then.

10–15 POINTS: You're cool, alright—cool as ice. And no cute pudgy dimples or doe eyes are going to melt away your nasty feelings toward the next generation. You are well within your rights to detest the young, but be forewarned: For reasons science has yet to explain, kids are drawn to your mean facade like fruit punch stains to a white, cotton blouse. If you don't loosen up a little, they may never give you peace.

Reality Check! The entertainment industry has a yen for making guys with babies seem funny, cool, and sexy, and many a single Cool Uncle has taken a nephew or niece to the park thinking it would help him score with the ladies. This could not be further from the truth. First off, nothing screams "unavailable" quite like a kid. As for real dads, overworked, under-rested, and covered in chunky vomit is a more accurate picture. Throw in the diaper bag and other accessories, and the snazzy dad starts to appear no more appetizing than a used wet wipe.

Put the X Back in Your Extra-Curricular Activities

Cultivating hobbies that are distasteful or off-limits to children practically ensures that your spare time will be enjoyed without the interference of OPCs. Here are some suggestions to get you started.

Wine tasting	Church	Conspiracy theorizing
Mushroom hunting	Storm chasing	Computer hacking
Chess	Bee farming	Slow art
Golf	Gardening	Collecting butterflies
Ornithology	Meditation	Art docent
Recreational stripping	The Theremin	Historic preservation
Genealogy	Breeding ferrets	Think tank
Ephemera society	Glassblowing	Board of directors
Book club	Sushi making	Soup kitchen volunteer
Music appreciation		

Playing It Cool, but Not Too Cool

A Cool Aunt or Uncle is one who's able not only to interface with the kid in the room but to charm her pretty pink booties off. If you have decided to go the cool route, though, you'll want to be cautious. It is possible to be too charismatic and wind up with a two-foot-tall, four-limbed parasite who clings to your legs from the second you arrive for the annual family barbecue. Yes, the line between Cool and Too Cool can be frustratingly thin at times, but these guidelines should help you stay the course, should you so choose. →

Cool is . . .

Squatting to make eye contact when you speak to a child.

Poking friendly fun at their parents; this makes you an ally in their battle for independence.

Sneaking them a little forbidden sugar.

Showing up with really great presents!

Being entertaining at birthday parties.

Asking about any imaginary friends they might be spending time with.

Talking to the child as you would an adult.

Letting the child pet and play with your cuddly canine and jump on your bed (shoeless, of course).

Too Cool is . . .

Compromising your chiropractic health with games like wrestling and horsey.

Revealing the fact that their mom was once known as "The Naked Party Queen of Piedmont High."

Sneaking the kid so much forbidden sugar that he morphs into a maniacal monkey.

Getting sucked into assembling those really great presents.

Dressing as a clown at their birthday party.

Telling them that your imaginary friend can beat up their imaginary friend.

Peppering your speech with taboo words.

Letting the child go anywhere near your designer coffee table or wine cellar.

Cool is . . .

Getting to know their entertainment choices. You don't have to like the latest hip-hop sensation, but you should at least know who he is.

Deferring to their coolness. Say, "Oh, you know far more about what's hip than your silly old Uncle Ralph."

Giving the sort of advice parents wish they could give but are afraid to, like, "Don't waste perfectly good booze. Alternate a glass of water for every beer to maintain that buzz all night!"

Being their confidante for the problems that are too embarrassing or tricky to bring to their parents.

Too Cool is . . .

Pretending to actually like that new reality show where co-eds try to pass for pimps.

Trying to convince them how cool you are by telling boring stories from your wild high school days.

Supplying alcohol or other substances.

Being their buddy. Face it, your wrinkles and jazz collection make you a huge social liability.

Lost in Translation

When friends have kids, one of the biggest changes you'll notice is how they speak. In addition to using new vocabulary words such as "goo goo ga-ga" and words that start with "w," as in "wittle baby woo woo," they'll also start replacing swearwords with a variety of substitutions. For the uninitiated, such language can be confusing, shocking, and even foul. While you're under no obligation to follow the rules, this guide to swearword substitution methods will help you translate what your formerly foul-mouthed pals are saying.

Swearword Substitution Method 1: Suffix Swap

First letter of naughty word, for example *f*, is tacked onto funny-sounding ending, like "lark" or "rick": "Flark! That's frickin' lame!"

Swearword Substitution Method 2: Sound Substitution

Swearword is replaced by similar-sounding word beginning with the same letter: "Shiitake! I burned the baby formula!"

Swearword Substitution Method 3: Foreign Frankness

Slang from another country is used in place of local vernacular. For example, the American "slut" becomes less offensive when spoken in British: "Your Cool Aunt was once a slag!" Brits, on the other hand, can replace words like "wanker" with the more American "jerk-off."

Swearword Substitution Method 4: Insertion

An extra syllable, such as "op," is inserted before vowels: "Scropew yopou, mopothoper fopuckoper!" Or the first letter of a word is placed at the end along with "ay": "Your teacher sounds like an itchbay!"

Swearword Substitution Method 5: Synonym Solution

Offensive word is simply replaced with a milder synonym: "Let's go kick some booty!"

Can't Stand Kids?

Even if you've decided that being a Cool Aunt or Uncle is not for you, you may want to disguise any negative feelings you have toward kids for one main reason: They can smell your fear. Once they've caught the scent, they will follow you, cling to your legs, tug at your belt straps, anything to get a rise out of you. Use psychological tactics to throw them off your trail.

Avoidance

Children can't torture you if they never see you. Plan adults-only time with the parents, who will appreciate the opportunity to leave the kid behind, if only for a few hours.

Pacification

Five minutes of your time freely and warmly given will more than make up for hours of interruptions and annoyance. Ask the child to show you a recent drawing or give a tour of her room. Say you're interested, but maintain emotional distance. The child will grow bored with you quickly enough.

Reverse Psychology

As soon as you see the child, demand that he kiss you on the cheek. (Wearing stinky lipstick or aftershave will make this extra unpleasant for the sensitive sprog.) Order the child to tell you all about his least favorite school subject. Check behind the ears for dirt, because "you care." Soon he will flee your unwelcome attention.

Negative Associations

Bring spinach bars and wheatgrass juice every time you visit the child. Act extremely offended when the child turns up her nose at these. Force her to take "just one bite. I swear you'll like it!" Be extra-chintzy with holiday and birthday gifts. Complain about your G.I. dysfunction in great detail.

OPC 101

For some unparents, holding a baby is still a treat. For others, it's anything but neat. As your friends and family become parents, they will inevitably ask you to perform parental tasks, from changing a baby's diapers to babysitting little Junior. Only you can draw the boundary between what you will and won't do when it comes to the OPCs in your life. This guide will assist you by showing you the right way to do things, and the right way to do things if you never, ever want to be asked to do those things again. *

BABYSITTING

The right way

Duck behind sofa and perform a puppet show using child's stuffed animals. Play peek-a-boo or a rousing game of Chutes and Ladders. Make fun, healthful snacks, like ants on a log (crunchy celery sticks stuffed with peanut butter and dotted with raisins).

The right way (if you never want to be asked again)

Prop child in clean, full litter box as close to television as possible. Raid the parents' refrigerator, liquor cabinet, music collection, etc.

PUTTING TO BED

The right way

Say, "time to go nighty-night." Dress tot in "jammies" and situate in bed with numerous soft pillows and stuffed animals. By dim light, read aloud from child's favorite book, such as *Aesop's Fables*. Don't forget to put the nightlight on before you leave.

The right way (if you never want to be asked again)

Place child on floor and cover with smelly blanket. Turn the lights out, put a flashlight under your chin, and read a terrifying story or sing a scary song. Feed child several glasses of milk to ensure bed-wetting. Fall asleep before the child.

The right way

Slip your arm beneath baby so baby's body is supported by your forearm and baby's head rests in the crook of your elbow. Coo and make goo-goo eyes.

The right way (if you never want to be asked again)

With one hand, grasp baby by an ankle and dangle upside down, arm outstretched so baby is as far from your body as possible.

*Note: Instructions on how to do things "the right way (if you never ever want to be asked to do these things again)" are intended for your amusement only. Do not, under any circumstances, follow this advice.

The right way

Wash hands thoroughly and remove soiled diaper carefully. Use baby wipes to clean baby's posterior, apply ointment if diaper rash is present, and sprinkle lightly with cornstarch to absorb wetness. Place baby's bottom atop back side of fresh diaper. Fold front side of diaper up toward tummy, then bring back sides around to meet the front. Secure snugly with sticky tabs.

The right way (if you never want to be asked again)

Remove soiled diaper and toss dirty side down onto floor. Place baby on fresh diaper, aligning baby's back with left leg hole. Seal off resulting gaps with duct tape and staples.

The right way

Place baby in high chair and secure bib snugly but not too tightly around baby's neck. Dip baby spoon into baby food, scooping up a pea-sized amount. Make choo-choo train noises and maneuver spoon to baby's lips. Repeat. Use edge of spoon to catch dribbles.

The right way (if you never want to be asked again)

P ace child on floor. Hand child a cooked steak. Stand back at a safe distance.

The right way

Clean "boo-boo" or "owie" gently with non-stinging antibacterial spray and cotton swabs, then apply soothing ointment. Cover affected area with bandage, preferably one featuring child's favorite cartoon character. Plant a gentle kiss onto the wounded area.

The right way (if you never want to be asked again)

Place child in bathtub and dribble a little hydrogen peroxide over the wound. Wait until screaming and bubbling subsides, then offer child a wad of toilet paper.

PLAYTIME AT THE PARK

The right way

Remain within five feet of child at all times. Place child into swing and gently push while saying "Wheeeeeeee!" Hold hands with child and reward yourselves with juice boxes on the way home.

The right way (if you never want to be asked again)

Using a leash and harness, secure child to jungle gym. Observe, while chain-smoking, from a park bench.

The right way

Wash hands thoroughly and warm a sterilized pacifier between your palms. Gently insert soft, rubbery tip into baby's mouth.

The right way (if you never want to be asked again)

Pour yourself a glass of wine and drink. Repeat until you no longer hear child's squalling. Offer baby the cork or, if you haven't finished it all, a little wine.

OPC Emergencies

If, heaven forbid, an emergency involving an OPC should happen on your watch, it won't do to be unprepared. In a pinch, refer to this handy guide and you'll always do the right thing. If all else fails, trust your instincts. They may not be nurturing, but that doesn't mean they're wrong.

Emergency	Action
Child reeks of poop, has wet substance running down leg, or says "I need to potty"	Hold child away from body and place into the arms of either an able-bodied parent or a running bath.
Ants in the pants are making child do the belly dance	Place child in a darkened, padded room filled with toys as well as a comfy bed. Lock the door and pray that the crash and ensuing nap come quickly.
Booger eating	Explain that boogers are in the same food group as broccoli, spinach, green beans, and peas, making them immediately distasteful to the child.
Baby barfs on your cashmere sweater	Take a big swill of wine, the redder the better, and slowly dribble it all over baby's new, white onesie.
Has bitten your leg	After scrubbing biter's arm with disinfectant soap, take it into your mouth. In between mouthfuls, say to the crying child, "How do you like it? Eh? Shoe's on the other foot now, isn't it? Mmmm. Delicious."
Dirt eating	Substitute dirt for cake mix and prepare a dessert of which no child will never ever ask for a second helping.
Throws temper tantrum	Immediately drop to the floor; lie on your back while dramatically kicking your legs and flinging your arms. Squeal like a raccoon in heat until the befuddled child is shocked into silence.

Off the Hook

Ten things you'll never be called upon to pay for.

1 Baby-food musher   2 Preschool tuition

3 The latest must-have sneakers

4 School or sport uniform   5 Ritalin prescription

6 Additional airplane seat

7 Braces

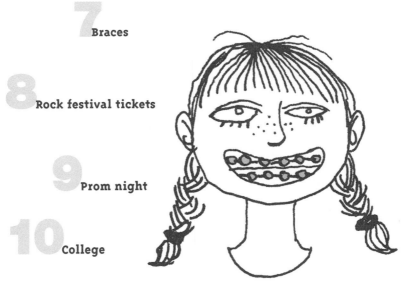

8 Rock festival tickets

9 Prom night

10 College

Diaper Diplomacy

It's not only the kids with whom you have to decide whether to be friends or foes. You'll have to make a call when it comes to the parents, as well. Obviously not every breeder turns into a total bore, but it only takes one to be a drag on your lifestyle. There is frankly no reason to remain friends with people who turn into Zombie Parents from the planet Zygote after having children. You should feel empowered to ditch losers who obsess over how many germs you might bring into their house, are afraid to trust babysitters, or talk endlessly about their offspring's banal achievements, as in, "Have I told you that Mommy's wittle woogie learned how to pull his pants down all by his wonesome today?" Here's how to get these family fanatics out of your life for good.

STEP ONE: Throughout the pregnancy or adoption process, barely acknowledge that they're going through this huge change. If they bring it up, say, "Oh, I forgot you two were having a little runt." Do not RSVP for the baby shower, but do show up near the tail end giftless and stinky from sweating it out at the gym.

STEP TWO: Whenever you speak to your soon-to-be-ex-friends, act oblivious to the fact that they've had a child. If they bring up how little sleep they're getting since little Max was born, pause and point out how exhausted you are from a wild weekend with the old party posse in Brooklyn. Be sure to sprinkle your long-winded anecdotes with, "You really had to be there."

STEP THREE: If they invite you over, take the opportunity to exhibit as many child-unfriendly behaviors as possible. After kissing the baby, remark that you hope your cold sore isn't contagious. Drink excessively and swear like a sailor in front of junior. If Dad asks you to hold the baby while he's using the restroom, snipe that you didn't sign up for household drudgery. Late in the evening, when Mom is clearly hinting that it's time for you to go home, insist that they should leave the kid at home unattended in the bathtub so you can all hit the clubs "like old times."

STEP FOUR: Congratulate yourself! You will never ever see these friends again. Rest assured you've been deleted from their nauseating photo-op holiday card mailing list and excised from the list of emergency contacts on the fridge next to the pureed squash stains and vaccination reminders.

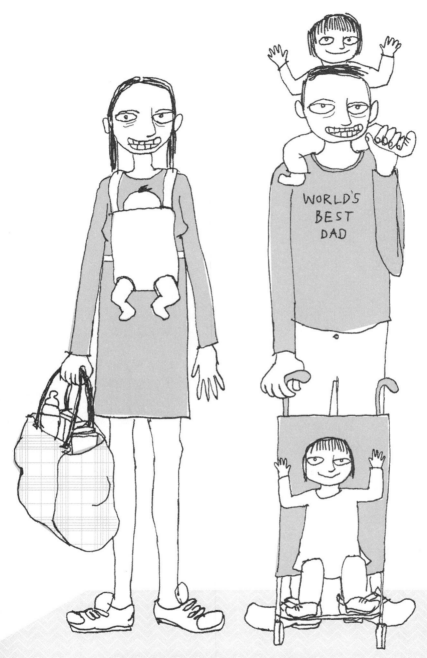

Zombie Parents from the planet Zygote

There's more than one way to make a baby.

The Meaning of Life

Making the most of your tot-free days

MANY PARENTS CLAIM that having children gives them a purpose in life. For unparents, finding meaning in life takes a little more creativity, intelligence, and verve than squeezing out a youngster, which, incidentally, anyone from your friendly neighborhood felon to the flea on your dog's behind to Albert Einstein can do. Indeed, there's simply no need to turn your entire life upside down and cast off your dreams like yesterday's teddy bear in order to give yourself a reason to get up in the morning.

FIRST YOU NEED to do some soul-searching to find that thing you've been placed on earth to do, be it writing a novel, saving your neighborhood park, finding a cure for the common cold, or simply cultivating a deep appreciation for the finer things in life. Because you have more time, income, and energy than parents, you'll find that accomplishing your goals is going to be a lot more feasible. Of course, our DNA has programmed us to make copies of ourselves, an urge that's hard to deny, especially after a couple of cocktails on an especially romantic date. Fortunately there are ways for you, as a childfree citizen, to ensure that your legacy continues long after you're pushing up the daisies, while making the most of your time on this hunk of rock as well.

Create, Don't Procreate

The urge to create is a natural one, though it's hard to fathom why so many choose to express it by making a child when there are so many perfectly wonderful alternatives. How will you expend all that excess creative energy you're not spending on finding ways to explain to junior that the chainsaw is not a toy? It all depends on what you want out of life!

If you're looking for . . .	Instead of having a kid, you could . . .
A rewarding long-term project	Create a monumental earthwork sculpture, discover the cure to cancer, or become the world's greatest trapeze artist.
A chance to impart your knowledge to others	Consider a career in TV punditry or street-corner preaching. Write frequent cranky letters to the editor of your local newspaper.
A way to save the world	You already have. By not having kids, you've saved the environment a lot of grief. Pat yourself on the back!

If you're looking for . . .	Instead of having a kid, you could . . .
Someone to take care of	Consider a sickly pet (try one with GI dysfunction or diabetes) or high-maintenance significant other.

A reason to wake up every morning	Move next door to a donut shop.
An excuse to drive a big car	Gain weight. Adopt a litter of dogs and drive them around with you. Take up a hobby that requires a lot of bulky equipment, like kayaking or snowboarding.

If you're looking for . . .	Instead of having a kid, you could . . .
A martyr complex	Set yourself an impossible goal like single-handedly eradicating homelessness in your lifetime. Become homeless yourself in the process.
Your very own Mini-Me	Donate your DNA to a cloning cult. Better yet, start your own cult and cultivate a following that will dress and act just like you.
A way to mold and shape the next generation	Teach junior high English at your local juvenile hall, or create your own vaguely psychedelic children's education program.
Something to look forward to when you're old	Start saving for your villa in Italy now and await the day when you can tell your boss, "Ciao!"
An interesting experience	Consider visiting a South American ayahuasca shaman. As with pregnancy, you will vomit, and afterward, many say, you will come into contact with the "architects of the universe."

If you're looking for . . .	Instead of having a kid, you could . . .
Somebody to love you unconditionally	Get a child substitute. (See pages 124–29 for suggestions.)
Someone to take care of you when you're old	Marry young.

BABY **NOT** ON BOARD

If da Vinci had been a dada

Making the Most of It

A parent's life is one long list of no-can-do's, while yours is a lengthy catalog of yes-I-cans! Don't wait until it's too late to make the most of your baby-free time on earth. If you haven't already, carpe diem, baby! These ideas should help get you started.

- Get a luxury degree.

- Become a doctor at age 50.

- Travel to far-flung locales.

- Take up a dangerous hobby like mushroom hunting.

- Frequent nude beaches.

- Leave your adult magazines out on the coffee table where they can be readily enjoyed.

- Build a wine cellar and don't forget to drink what's in it!

- Go on a weeklong bender now and then. Don't forget to ask your co-workers with kids to pick up the slack for you.

- Become so spiritual that children are no longer able to penetrate your eerie, wide-eyed calm.

- Get waxed where no wax has gone before.

- Have a torrid, romantic affair with someone completely inappropriate.

- Pull an all-nighter every once in a while just to prove you still got it.

- On Friday morning, book a flight to Paris arriving on Saturday.

- Get arrested for a good cause.

- Dine regularly on blowfish sushi and other potentially fatal delicacies.

- Dress "young" for your age.

- Run for school board (just to freak out all the parents).

- Moon a school bus of teenagers.

- Learn how to ride a motorcycle.

Anti Grave-ity Matter

Ten reasons you'll look younger than all your friends with grandkids.

1. You've consistently gotten 8 hours of sleep per night.

2. There's always been room in your lifestyle for healthy habits, like unicycling.

3. No teens out past curfews means fewer worry lines.

4. Not breastfeeding has given you buoyant boobies.

5. Balancing work and family never took its toll on you.

6. You haven't gone deaf while chaperoning your kids to Suck-a-palooza.

7 People who are having fun generally look younger.

8 You haven't cracked any brittle bones while lifting grandkids.

9 You've got more disposable income to spend on looking hot.

10 There are no young people around to make you feel old.

Reality Check! What else is having a child than an opportunity to create something new, mold and shape it, then step back and see how it turns out? It's no different than writing a novel, knitting a scarf, or painting a scene from your favorite park. Of course, if the novel is a stinker, the scarf a fashion disaster, the painting not worth five cents at a yard sale, no harm done, right? But a child-rearing endeavor gone wrong? Well, that's something the parent will have to live with—literally live with, as in 35-year-old unemployed son sleeping on the couch and bringing his dumb buddies over to throw burnt toasts at the TV all day while you're working your butt off to make ends meet, live with—for the rest of his or her life. Sure, if things go right, the parent might also enjoy a lifetime of self-congratulatory bliss. But in creative pursuits, there are no guarantees.

If Beethoven had bred

Retirement Boosters

The children may be the future, but by not having kids your future is a whole lot brighter. Just imagine what you could have if you invest what a parent spends on one aspect of having one child over the course of 18 years.

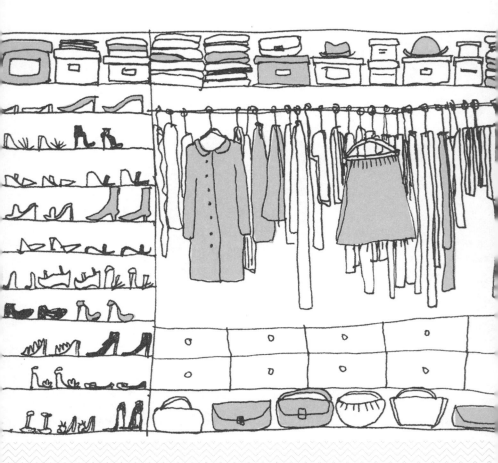

With the money you would spend on 18 years of the kid's . . .	In 18 years you could . . .
Housing	Buy a vacation home.
Food	Get really into experimental airplanes.
Transportation	Fulfill your need for speed by purchasing a fabulous hot rod.
Clothing	Give your wardrobe a complete makeover.
Health care	Have a cosmetic surgeon lift 15 years off your face.
Child care and education	Donate to your alma mater and get an honorary doctorate in exchange.
Misc. expenses	Sail around the world in first-class accommodations.
All of the above	Retire sooner than later.

The Golden Years

Ah, the golden years, the time in life when you can really relax, kick back, and enjoy the fruits of your hard work. While parents obviously look forward to this part of life as well, the autumn and winter of your life will be all the more rich and rewarding thanks to your decision not to breed. Here are ten things you can look forward to that they can't:

1 Retiring early enough to actually enjoy it, thanks to all the orthodontia, ski trips, and prom nights you never had to pay for.

2 Spoiling yourself—not a bunch of whiny grandkids—rotten when the holidays roll around.

3 Without grandkids to keep tabs on, you can settle down anywhere you please, even if it's in a pimped-out RV complete with a thumping stereo system and heart-shaped waterbed.

4 While gramps and granny waste precious hours of their retirement waiting in line for a kiddy ride at Disneyland, you'll be staking out the perfect wave in Australia.

5 That casino waitress with the giant jugs may not seem like a love connection, but you know she's going to take extra-special care of you when you're too old to stir your own martinis.

6 You'll never suffer the humiliation of mixing up the grandkids' diapers with your own.

7 You can will your entire life savings to the Water Buffalo Appreciation Society and nobody's going to make a stink about it.

8 Nobody will bat an eyelid when you dye your hair blue on purpose.

9 You won't get saddled with the kids when their mom and dad join a commune in India.

10 If retirement gets boring, you can always follow the Rolling Stones tour around for a while.

BABY NOT ON BOARD

If Julia Child had had a bun in her oven

Forget-You-Nots

Want to be remembered after you've croaked? With no kids to leave flowers at your gravesite, you're better off spending that money on something people will see.

ARBOR DAME

Arrange to have a lovely garden or bower cultivated in the park of your choice with prominent signage bearing your name.

SEAT OF HONOR

Provide a bench along a favorite fitness trail upon which people can rest their weary bottoms. The plaque bearing your name will let them know who to thank.

THE [YOUR NAME HERE] COLLECTION

Donate artwork or collectables you've curated over the years to a worthy museum when you can collect no more.

HOUSEHOLD NAME

Make your home so bizarre and freaky that people will be compelled to turn it into a kitschy museum after you've taken up your heavenly zip code.

MONIKER HALL

Donate enough money so that a new wing of a library or an updated chemistry lab at your alma mater will bear your name.

BILLY THE NO-KIDS

Live your life with such dazzling aplomb that your name becomes a slang word for "wacky nonbreeder."

STREET CRED

Pull some strings down at City Hall so that a street in a new subdivision is named after you.

IN THE STARS

Pay to have an asteroid or comet named in your honor.

Mother Earth Thanks You

Thanks to your wise decision not to have kids, here are some of the things you won't leave for future generations to deal with:

- More than 10,000 non-biodegradable poopy diapers

- Twice your own carbon dioxide emissions

- 52 tons of garbage

- Several dozen mercury- and lead-filled computer husks

- An even bigger hole in the ozone layer

And here are some things you will make available:

- 2000 barrels of oil

- 10 million gallons of potable water

- Hundreds of acres of forests

- Fewer traffic jams

- Less urban sprawl

The Childfree Way to Spread Your DNA

The longing for immortality, for some piece of yourself to live on long after you have shuffled off your mortal coil, is universal. And children, bearing as they do one's genetic code and annoying habits, are an easy and obvious way to make sure you never truly go completely bye-bye. But if you're really concerned about leaving a little piece of yourself behind after you're dead, there are far easier—or at least more unique—ways than having a child or three.

THE GIFT OF EGG/SPERM

WHAT IS IT? If you need to ask . . .

HOW LONG WILL IT LAST? Provided your donation is used to make some infertile, baby-craving family extremely happy and the offspring doesn't meet an untimely end, then 76 years or so.

WILL IT HURT? As with birth, if you are male, the answer is no; if you are female, most assuredly.

WHAT WILL MY LEGACY BE? This is a great way to have a child without ever having to raise the little bugger. Your DNA gets passed along, meanwhile you get to keep your childfree lifestyle. It's a win-win!

COST? If you're lucky, you could make money off of this.

ORGAN DONATION

WHAT IS IT? Upon brain death, all your healthy organs are ripped from your body and gently placed in another.

HOW LONG WILL IT LAST? However long the recipient survives.

WILL IT HURT? Whatever got you to the state of being able to give your organs probably hurt a lot, but once you're there, it's as painless as petting a soft kitten.

WHAT WILL MY LEGACY BE? Organ donors are granted hero status. This Pollyanna act makes the most out of your own death by turning it into a second chance on life for somebody else.

COST? Free to you, priceless to the recipient.

OBJECT LESSON

WHAT IS IT? After you're dead, your body is donated for the purposes of educating future doctors.

HOW LONG WILL IT LAST? How long does formaldehyde last?

WILL IT HURT? No, but it is kind of creepy to imagine your dead naked self being ogled by a bunch of strangers in scrubs and masks.

WHAT WILL MY LEGACY BE? The downside is your DNA will eventually get flushed down a medical waste disposal, but the lessons learned will improve the lives of everyone touched by the doctors who studied your body.

COST? Free to you, priceless to the future of humanity.

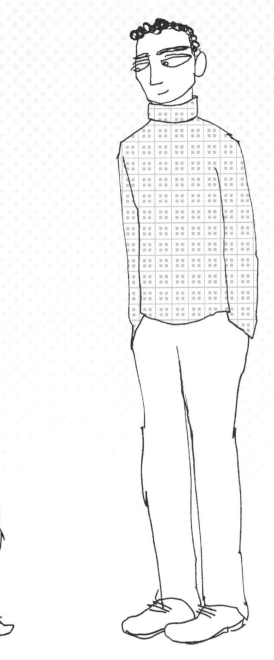

Why settle for kids when you could have a clone?

CRYOGENIC FREEZING

WHAT IS IT? Having your body frozen to -120° Celsius just after your heart stops and stored in a high-security facility until a nanoscientist discovers a cure for death and a way to regenerate cells.

HOW LONG WILL IT LAST? You could wake up in 20 years or 20,000 years.

WILL IT HURT? Coming back to life could hurt a little.

WHAT WILL MY LEGACY BE? A number of possibilities exist. You and your decrepit body could return for a second life on earth sometime in the next millennium, or you could be an expensive popsicle for all eternity.

COST? Expensive.

MINI-YOU

WHAT IS IT? A sample of DNA obtained from your blood is stored until the time human-cloning becomes practical.

HOW LONG WILL IT LAST? Depends on how skilled your future cloning scientists are.

WILL IT HURT? Just a quick stick and you're through.

WHAT WILL MY LEGACY BE? The stuff of science fiction and tabloid fodder!

Your DNA will be used to create a clone of your former self. Why have a child, when you're perfect just as you are? Alas, things might go horribly wrong and you'll go down in history as the clone with internal organs growing out of his leg.

COST? The price of one doctor's visit to obtain the DNA sample and long-term, sanitary storage.

The family that dines together whines together.

Doubt-Busters

Tips and encouragement to keep you strong

WHEN PARENTS have doubts about whether they've made the right decision, there's only one thing they can do: lock those feelings up in the dankest, darkest dungeon of their soul and throw away the key because that baby isn't going away any time soon. When unparents have misgivings, on the other hand, they can explore a whole host of options ranging from pricey psychotherapy to reaffirming their freedom with a raucous trip to the Bahamas or adopting a friendly child substitute.

QUESTIONING YOUR decision not to rear a child is only natural in a society where parenthood is viewed as the norm and everything else is deemed psycho. You're bound to feel like the odd one out now and then and to wonder why that is. Fortunately, you don't have a squalling infant to compete with those private moments of reflection and self-exploration that help you confirm that you've been right about this not-breeding thing all along.

Quiz: What Are You Really Craving?

Do you really need a whole child to chase the baby blues away, or will a warm, cuddly gerbil do the trick? Knowing what you're really craving will help you find the perfect child substitute to make those ridiculous urges go bye-bye.

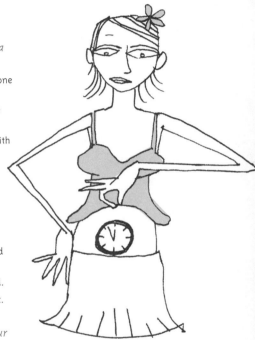

1 *What do you feel when you see a sweet, brown-eyed pony?*

A) The overpowering urge to give someone a hug.

B) Like I want to adopt the sweet, fragile wittle guy.

C) What does this question have to do with me?

D) Giddddyap!!!!

2 *Do you have a biological clock?*

A) Only in my groin area and it's purely recreational.

B) Yes, and I can hear it ticking loud and clear.

C) If I did, I'd have it surgically removed.

D) I like to rock out to its persistent beat.

3 *How do you tend to care for your body?*

A) I pamper it rotten with massages, baths, and spa treatments.

B) Health foods, exercise, frequent check-ups, vitamins . . .

C) Whatever it takes to look hot.

D) Dodgeball!!!

4 *Which best describes the plant life currently in your home?*

A) Flowers, cut and displayed in a vase.

B) A garden of greenery in need of frequent watering.

C) Plastic or edible is all I have time for.

D) The kind you inhale.

5 *How do you remember the happier moments of your childhood?*

A) A sunlight-dappled, soft-focused dreamy time.

B) Blissfully carefree.

C) The only time in my life when I've truly been the center of attention.

D) Recess.

6 *Which of the following reasons for not having babies do you most relate to?*

A) They smell like butt.

B) There are already so many kids in the world. Why add another?

C) Once they become teenagers, they hate you and ignore everything you say.

D) They hog all the good toys.

7 *Which secret passion would you be most likely to follow?*

A) A star-crossed romance.

B) Making the world a better place.

C) Fame, riches, and power, for starters.

D) A spot on the latest competitive reality TV show.

8 *You're having lunch with a friend when his baby starts crying. What do you do?*

A) Blow kisses at baby in hope that it will quiet down once it feels the love.

B) Quickly locate the pacifier and shut the poor thing up!

C) Complain loudly that your foie gras is being spoiled by the racket.

D) Put on an extended stand-up routine that's sure to shake baby out of his depression.

9 *Which song would be most fitting on the soundtrack to your life?*

A) "Don't You Want Somebody to Love" (Jefferson Airplane)

B) "I'll Be There for You" (Rembrants; *Friends* theme song)

C) "I'm Too Sexy" (Right Said Fred)

D) "Girls Just Wanna Have Fun" (Cyndi Lauper)

10 *Which adjective are you most likely to use to describe kids?*

A) Doughy

B) Needy

C) Parasitic

D) Playmate

SCORING: Create four columns for A, B, C, and D answers. Make a mark under A for every A answer, a mark under B for every B answer, and so on. When you are done, count and write down the totals for each.

IF MOST OF YOUR ANSWERS ARE As: You are a lover, not a breeder! You adore romance, beauty, passion. You have so much love in your heart and so much room to receive love it's only natural that you might think that a baby could help out. But if you suspect that babies only love you unconditionally for a while then grow old and blame your many failings as a parent for all their problems, then you would be onto something. Babies don't love; they need. Cultivating a deep and abiding self love or indulging in a great romance should take care of any persistent baby cravings you feel. Consider sending Valentine's Day cards every year in lieu of the usual holiday dreck.

IF MOST OF YOUR ANSWERS ARE Bs: You feel the need to nurture. Problems? You want to fix them. People? You want to help them. And who is needier than a whiny, smelly, helpless wittle woo-woo gotchems? Nobody, that's who. But can't your need to be needed—to be helpful, meaningful, and heroic—be satisfied by less drastic means than giving birth or adopting? In fact it can! You don't need no stinkin' baby. You need a cause, a purpose—be it the environment, the whales, the squirrels, reinstating smoking in bars, tofu pride.

IF MOST OF YOUR ANSWERS ARE Cs: You are a rock star, a supernova, a charismatic leader, the glowing center of your very own universe. Now a child would certainly be an adoring addition to your fan base. But once it hits ohhhhh sayyyy, 12, the kiddo would in fact go out of her way to avoid you and pretend like you don't exist—a serious ego bruiser, to say the least. A dog's devotion, on the other hand, never fades. And if that's not enough, consider leading a company, a movement, a congregation, a polka band. The spotlight is yours for the taking; don't let some little tyke steal your limelight.

IF MOST OF YOUR ANSWERS ARE Ds: Hey, Peter Pan, that baby you're craving is not a playmate. As a parent you're expected to not only have fun with your kid but set an example, lay down the law, discipline, pay the bills, pin the poor thing to the examination table during vaccinations, cook dinner, clean up after dinner, change diapers, wash bottles, and oh how the list of hard work goes on. Undoubtedly the kids in your life are drawn to you like gum to a rubber sole, which might make you wonder whether you shouldn't take the plunge and plop out a little buddy of your own. Resist the temptation and continue being the uber-Cool Aunt or Uncle that you are. You do it so well!

IF IT'S TOO CLOSE TO CALL: You're more complex than a crib-assembly instruction manual! When you think about having kids, you tend to see all sides and, perhaps, have a difficult time discerning how you really feel. But imagine how little time you'd have to contemplate and philosophize on deep topics once a kid entered your life. Without kids you can waffle and flip-flop as long as you please. Consider thinking through your thoughts and feelings on procreating to be one of your many lifelong endeavors.

Dog vs. Baby

No matter why you're feeling baby-yearning, having an appropriate child substitute can help to quell your desires. And of all the child substitutes available to unparents such as yourself, none is more similar to the real deal than dogs. They require almost as much time, money, and attention as children. In fact, as this side-by-side comparison shows, glue some fur onto a toddler and add a tail and you're basically looking at a really weird dog, though with some key differences. For example, a dog won't grow into an angry, money-sucking teenager, whereas a baby most certainly will.

BABY	CANINE CHILD SUBSTITUTE
AVERAGE LIFESPAN: 76 years	**AVERAGE LIFESPAN:** 15 years
PHYSICAL ATTRIBUTES:	**PHYSICAL ATTRIBUTES:**
• Teethes	• Sharp teeth
• Covered in bacteria	• Covered in bacteria
• Smells like talcum and doo-doo	• Smells like dog shampoo and doo-doo
• Opposable thumbs, harbingers of destruction	• Tail frequently knocks things over
• Oozing out of orifices	• Oozing out of orifices
BEHAVIORS:	**BEHAVIORS:**
• Wakes up several times throughout the night	• Wakes up early in the morning
• Cries loudly and often	• Howls
• Poops at inconvenient times	• Poops at inconvenient times
• Embarrasses you by throwing temper tantrums in public	• Embarrasses you by humping other dogs at the dog park
• Really likes milk	• Really likes rotting animal carcasses
• Chases cats	• Chases cats
CAPABILITIES:	**CAPABILITIES:**
• Screams and cries to get its way	• Gives you big, sad, wet, round puppy eyes to get its way
• Can be walked on a leash	• Can be walked on a leash
• Gradually becomes an independent adult	• Remains in a permanent state of childlike dependence
• Not potty trainable for 2½ years	• Potty trainable from the get-go

BABY

INCAPABILITIES:

* Cannot fix own dinner
* Cannot bathe own self
* Cannot tell you what's wrong
* Cannot clean up own mess

CARE REQUIREMENTS:

* Must not be left alone under any circumstances
* Diapers need changing 5–12 times per day
* Proximity to a park or playground is essential
* Must be wiped down hourly (if not more often)
* Requires constant exposure to primary colors

MISC:

* Once yours, it cannot be given back
* Landlord-friendly
* Useful as an excuse for not doing things like working late, attending parties, or "letting yourself go"

COSTS: $1 million dollars, plus your sanity

CANINE CHILD SUBSTITUTE

INCAPABILITIES:

* Cannot fix own dinner
* Cannot bathe itself
* Cannot tell you what's wrong
* Can bury dead squirrel in your backyard

CARE REQUIREMENTS:

* Can be left alone for up to 8 hours!
* Requires regular walks with the pooper scooper
* Proximity to a dog park is essential
* Monthly trips to fur stylist (a.k.a. "groomer") recommended
* Demands frequent exposure to smelly socks

MISC:

* Can be returned or exchanged for a newer model
* Landlord-unfriendly
* Will force you to go outside and get some fresh air at least twice per day, if not more

COSTS: $10,000 over lifetime

Non-Canine Child Substitutes

Discerning eyes may have picked up on just how similar a dog is to a baby. If you're understandably shy of taking on such a huge commitment, perhaps you'll want to try a different type of child substitute. Fortunately a wide range of options are available for the adopting. Here are just a few popular ones.

Birds

SIMILARITIES: Require recurrent feeding and cleaning; squawk frequently

DIFFERENCES: Are perfectly content to pass their days in a cage

CHALLENGE LEVEL: Medium

Computers

SIMILARITIES: Highly recommended that you teach them how to do things and check frequently for viruses; suck up many hours of your day

DIFFERENCES: About as warm and cuddly as a stone sarcophagus

CHALLENGE LEVEL: Low to high, depending on worms

Gardens

SIMILARITIES: Won't thrive unless you constantly perform numerous mindless, time-consuming tasks (i.e., seeding, weeding, fertilizing)

DIFFERENCES: If you screw things up, they still won't murder you in your sleep.

CHALLENGE LEVEL: Medium

Geezers

SIMILARITIES: Require spoon feeding, diaper changes, and hand-holding when crossing streets; fragile immune system

DIFFERENCES: Much larger and more expensive than a baby; may leave you a fortune in exchange for your kindness

CHALLENGE LEVEL: High

Hot Rod

SIMILARITIES: Fun to show off; attractive to some chicks; and costly to fuel, maintain, and pamper

DIFFERENCES: Only makes noise when you press on horn or rev the engine

CHALLENGE LEVEL: Low

Your Inner Child

SIMILARITIES: Lives to have fun; occasionally throws a tantrum and gets nostalgic for *The Muppet Show*

DIFFERENCES: Able to stay up well past midnight; takes personal pride in feeding and dressing self

CHALLENGE LEVEL: Medium

Cats

SIMILARITIES: Quickly become indifferent to you once they've reached a certain age

DIFFERENCES: Self-cleaning and capable of being trained to use a toilet (really)

CHALLENGE LEVEL: High

Nieces/Nephews

SIMILARITIES: Are actual bona fide children

DIFFERENCES: Typical commitment lasts only a few hours at a time; don't require discipline (from you, at least)

CHALLENGE LEVEL: Medium

Students

SIMILARITIES: Are often bona fide children; expect you to teach them something useful

DIFFERENCES: You don't have to teach them everything, and you get paid for the time you spend with them.

CHALLENGE LEVEL: High

Carnivorous Plants

SIMILARITIES: Must be hand-fed protein and purified water at regular intervals; eat bugs

DIFFERENCES: Never talk back, cry, or sulk

CHALLENGE LEVEL: Low

Ten Fail-Proof Ways to Nix No-Natal Depression

Even if you love your child substitute more than anything, there may still be times when you feel left out from the rest of the breeding world. When such thoughts arise, don't throw your contraceptives into the dumpster. Here are ten ways to remind yourself of all that you're not missing.

1 Take a field trip to your local reusable diaper service. Breathe deeply.

2 Go to the Web site Google.com and click on Images. Search for "birth + crowning."

3 Spend a week raising a "Baby Think It Over," the lifelike doll used by sex ed programs to convince teenagers that birth control is cooler than the alternative.

4 Obtain an alarm clock with a recording device. Use it to capture the sound of a traumatized infant. Set it to wake you up to the sound of baby screams every two hours.

5 Have you ever taken a good look at maternity clothes, especially the pants and undies?

6 Place your most prized possession on the sidewalk outside the local high school one Monday morning. Don't retrieve it until after 5 PM. Imagine doing this daily with your very own teenager.

7 When planning your next vacation, calculate what it would cost to buy one extra of everything.

Your Underwear

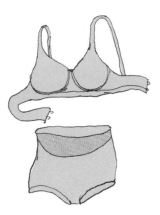

Your Underwear with Kids

8 If you are female, take a medium sized melon and hold it up to your privates. Visualize what it would feel like to get that thing up in there, or rather, out.

9 Go to a popular, kid-friendly pizza parlor. Every time you hear a baby cry, run to the bathroom and splash some milk onto your nipples.

10 Test the urine and feces levels of your local public swimming pool several minutes after kids' hour has ended. If this isn't gross enough, jump in and do a few laps in this murky swamp of human waste.

Under Pressure!

One of the reasons unparents occasionally feel the urge to have kids is that society is constantly telling them that they ought to want kids. Whether it's your parents, your co-workers, friends, or just the commercials on TV who are turning the screws—once you reach a certain age, get married, or so much as look like you might be fertile, you're bound to start feeling the heat. Here are some easy avoidance strategies you may want to try.

Creative Censorship

Just say no to "lifestyle" magazines that include fun crafts you can do with your kids, daytime television and its bevy of fabric softener and floor wax ads, and family-based sitcoms, which make it all seem like a bucket of laughs.

Selective Socializing

When getting together with friends who have babies, do something at night and without the little monsters when they'll be much more likely to talk about how relieved they are to take a break from junior than how blissful being a parent is. Ditch pals who become Parent Zombies (see page 90).

Snitty Repartee

Politely excuse yourself from water-cooler conversations that veer onto the subject of kids, or interrupt with a similar story about the dead mouse your feline child substitute gave you the other day. "Even though it was dead, that mouse was so cute. And you should see how little Lulu was playing with its corpse! I'm so proud of her."

Lie Like a Rugrat

When asked about your future baby plans, allude to something tragic in your past that makes having children impossible. Rather than risk standing by helplessly while the whole tragic

tale unfurls from your lips, people will stop pressing and run like hell to less taboo shores.

Put Fido on a Pedestal

Refer to child substitutes as your "babies," and do all the things that parents do with their kids, including framing their dorky portraits, taking trips to the park, bragging about accomplishments, and complaining about the lack of good, affordable, available babysitters.

Love and Marriage, Sans the Baby Carriage

For some people, the realization that they don't want to have children comes after they've already paired up with that special someone. When one partner wants kids and the other doesn't, it can create a serious rift in the relationship. But it doesn't have to. Rather than trying to persuade your partner to forgo kids, let these situations do the convincing for you.

MOVIE NIGHT FROM HELL: The popcorn has popped. The couch is prepped for snuggling. Oops! Did you forget to mention that tonight's special feature is a romantic natural birthing video? Just think, that could be you some day!

WHINE AND DINE: Dinner is on you! Hope your date is up for a six o'clock seating at the family-friendly restaurant of your choice. Be on guard for flying French fries.

TROUBLE FEATURE: Talk about horror movies! Many cinemas now offer special matinees for folks with babies. Take your mate to one of these showings. If he complains about not being able to hear the dialogue above all the squalling, shrug and say, "I didn't think you'd mind!"

DATE DOWNERS: Whenever doing anything fun together, whether it's a fancy dinner, a weekend getaway, a challenging hike, or a couples' massage, don't neglect to mention, "Once we have kids, we won't get to do this anymore."

WILD WEEKEND: If all else fails, go for total immersion. Offer to take care of someone else's kid for an entire weekend. Will there be sex? Not likely. Morning snuggles? As if! What about reading the newspaper? Ha ha ha ha! Nope, it's just going to be you, your honey, and one squalling, hyperactive little munchkin to look after until Sunday night.

BUDGETARY BLUES: Make a budget. Be sure to put all the things your significant other especially enjoys near the top—including CDs, red wine, dry cleaning, lingerie, massages, sushi, shoes, lattes, and salon haircuts—then cross them off using bold red ink. When she asks why, shrug and say, "Oh, I was just thinking ahead to when we have kids."

Procreative Contradictions

Parents will try to convince you that their life is better for having children, but they also complain constantly about how robbed they feel. Which version do you believe?

This Could Be Heaven	This Could Be Hell
"Having kids has really helped me find myself."	"Since little Edie was born, I haven't read a thing."
"Being a parent is so rewarding."	"We haven't rewarded ourselves with a vacation since Kylie came into our lives."
"Kids sure do keep you on your toes!"	"I just can't seem to lose those extra 40 pounds I gained during my pregnancy."
"It's the most fulfilling job I've ever done."	"I never have time for myself anymore."
"Birth is magical."	"I grunted like a dying sow for 20 of the most hideously painful hours of my entire life."
"It opens up a whole new part of your relationship."	"When was the last time we made whoopee? Ha ha ha ha haaaaa ha ha ha! As if."
"You really learn what's important in life after you have kids."	"I'd cut off my right leg just to sleep in once, just once dear god, on a Saturday."
"It's different when they're yours."	"I miss the good old days when I could hand the child back."

Reality Check! Why does everybody assume that there's this biological clock buried deep inside everyone that's just waiting to go off? Many people never feel the need to breed at all, yet they are told that someday that imaginary tick-tocking will commence and they'll suddenly feel their life won't be complete without babies. When confronted with needling questions about your own so-called clock, it's often useful to counter with scientific probing: Now where is this clock located again? What does it look like? Does it secrete hormones or is it more of a processing center? Is it vestigial? If removed, what effect will that have on the functioning of my body? That should end the discussion fairly quickly.

More Quick Replies for on the Fly

Parents have plenty of reasons for why they chose to have kids, but that doesn't mean their reasons should apply to you. When they try to feed you a line, spit back a quick reply.

REASON FOR HAVING KIDS: It gives you a reason to get up in the morning.
REBUTTAL: Coffee and a shower do the trick for me.

REASON FOR HAVING KIDS: They make you a better person.
REBUTTAL: Better than whom?

REASON FOR HAVING KIDS: I have so much love to give.
REBUTTAL: Get a room!

REASON FOR HAVING KIDS: It's made our relationship stronger.
REBUTTAL: Really? I'd think sharing my bed with an underaged third person would have the opposite effect.

REASON FOR HAVING KIDS: I thought I would regret not doing it.
REBUTTAL: I totally relate. I often regret not trying heroin.

REASON FOR HAVING KIDS: Someone to take care of me when I'm old.
REBUTTAL: Have you met my houseboy Roger? He gives great foot rubs.

REASON FOR HAVING KIDS: My life would be empty without them.
REBUTTAL: My social life would be empty with them.

REASONS FOR HAVING KIDS: Somebody to pass along all my wisdom to.
REBUTTAL: Every serial killer's parent probably said the same thing once.

Perks

If they think you're missing out because you don't have kids, just think of all the things they no longer get to enjoy.

- Sleeping in
- Late-night TV
- Rock concerts
- Sanity
- Shakespeare
- Four-letter words
- Four-syllable words
- Friday nights
- R-rated movies
- Veggies

- Vino
- Astonishingly expensive shoes
- Spontaneous after-work martinis
- Peace and quiet
- Five minutes without interruption
- Adult conversation
- Loft living
- Being cooler than all your friends with kids

- Long, leisurely vacations
- Breakfast at 11, dinner at 9
- Personal aspirations
- Sexy swimsuits
- Not relating to your parents
- Social smoking
- Zippy convertibles

Childfree Loves Company

Families have support groups, get-togethers, therapists, and like-minded friends that they can turn to for support, and so should you. Try these group activities when you want to celebrate your own wonderful choice.

CALLING ALL CHILDFREE PEOPLE

Start or join a childfree social club. This is an especially good idea for singles, or couples whose friends are breeding like bunnies. Make sure to fill the evening with things parents no longer get to enjoy, like really long backrubs and raunchy jokes.

TAKE BACK THE DAY

Has your favorite restaurant been overrun by tots? Has the local park become a watering hole for the diapered set? Don't just stand by and let them ruin it. Descend on the place with a posse of foulmouthed unparents and scare all the families away.

MAKE FUN OF BREEDERS

Venting is important. Every once in a while get together with like-minded no-creators and let 'em rip! Mock comedians who turn soft once they become parents. Hurl insults at your friends who've turned into Parent Zombies. Exchange colorful anecdotes about OPCs from hell. Beat your chest and moan about how baby-centric the world is becoming. Let it out, then have a martini. You deserve it.

MAKE A DIFFERENCE

Organize letter-writing campaigns to fight policies that promote overpopulation. Build a Web site to provide support to unparents around the globe. Volunteer and show the world that you don't need kidlettes to have a social conscience.

Clip and Save Affirmations

Carry these with you in your wallet or tape them to your
bathroom mirror to give you encouragement on a daily
basis.

My DNA belongs to nobody but me.

No child could ever be as hot as I am right now.

If I had kids, I'd be weeping right now.

My life is too good to share with anyone else.

Earth has 10,000 fewer rotting diapers thanks to me.

I will never sound just like my mother or father.

---

*My sense of well-being is not determined by how
well Susie did in swim class today.*

No kid with the chicken pox is going to mess up my career.

I'm so creative I don't need to procreate.

I'm a slave to no one. OK. Maybe fashion.

Afterword

Changing your mind without losing face

ONE OF the biggest benefits of being childfree is the fact that you have the ability to change your mind. While it's difficult to understand why anyone would want to give up all the wonderful benefits of being childfree, at least you'll be doing so fully aware of the monumental costs.

THE BOTTOM LINE is and always has been: It's your choice. If you decide to switch gears and become a parent, at least you can say you lived your childfree years to the fullest, that your unparenting days were among the best in your life.

OF COURSE, changing one's mind after touting the wonders of your brilliant childfree lifestyle to the world can be a touch embarrassing. It's definitely recommended that you break the news slowly, starting with small hints that gradually progress into an announcement. Adopting a child, particularly one from a developing nation, is a good way to start a family without trampling all over your stance on the environment and overpopulation. Plus, everyone will be so in awe of your good deed they'll forget you ever mockingly referred to them as "stupid breeders."

Good luck!

Resources

Links to organizations, information, and support groups to help you on your merry childfree way

Boost Your Morale

Childfree by Choice

A compendium of unparenting resources, news, chat rooms, and other fun stuff.
www.childfreebychoice.com

The Childfree-By-Choice Pages

A directory of books, Web sites, and other information helpful to people of the unfamily persuasion.
www.childfree.net

Childfree Heroes

A big list of famous people who've skipped having kids.
www.suite101.com/
article.cfm/6392/58081

Unruly, Ill-Mannered Yard Apes

A delightful assemblage of baby synonyms (for example, sperm vermin), childfree haikus, and other entertainments.
www.tumalo.com/
unruly.htm

The Childfree Ring

Links, links, and more links to a ton of Web sites and organizations.
www.ringsurf.com/netring?
ring=childfree;action=list

Socialize

No Kidding

An international social club for folks who've chosen not to procreate.
www.nokidding.net

Yahoo Childfree Dating E-mail List

Where the childfree meet and chat.
www.groups.yahoo.com/
group/Childfree_Singles

International Child-free Meetup

Go to the site and type in your zip code to find like-minded people to hang out with.
www.childfree.meetup.com

Childfree Personals

Connect to a whole world of single nonbreeders.
www.cfpersonals.com/
cf_index.php

Express Yourself

You Still Have a Choice

This message board provides a forum for unparents to engage in mutual support.
www.fred.net/turtle/kids/
kids2.html

The LivingFree Bulletin

People who post to this list are encouraged to express intelligent, well-reasoned thoughts on not having kids.
www.dork.com/livingfree

Brats

A message board that encourages unparents to post their meanest reactions.
www.fred.net/turtle/kids/
kidrants.shtml

Positively Childfree

A message board that encourages unparents to post their warmest, fuzziest thoughts.
www.positivelychildfree.com

Spread Your DNA

Cyrogenic Freezing

The official Web site for Alcor Life Extension Foundation, which cryogenically freezes corpses in order to, maybe, one day bring them back to life.
www.alcor.org

The Human Cloning Foundation

Learn everything you wanted to know about having yourself cloned in the future from this helpful Web site.
www.humancloning.org

Organ Donation

Documentary-style storytelling plus links and other information on passing along the gift of life once you're through with yours.
www.organtransplants.org

So You Wanna Donate Sperm?

Everything you need to know about how.
www.soyouwanna.com/site/syws/sperm/sperm.html

So You Wanna Donate Eggs?

Read all about how to do it here.
www.eggdonor.com

See the World

The Curmudgeon's Guide to Child-Free Travel: Exactly How and Precisely Where to Enjoy Idyllic Grownup Getaways, by Jennifer Lawler. The must-have guide to getting away from it all—especially children.

Get Active

Population Connection

Formerly Zero Population Growth, this organization encourages people to have fewer children in order to have a sustainable world.
www.population connection.org

Negative Population Growth

This membership-based organization urges people not to reproduce in order to bring the population back to sustainable levels.
www.npg.org

World Childfree Organization

This international nonprofit organization s dedicated to spreading the message of childfree bliss to the rest of the planet.
www.worldchildfree.org

Kidding Aside

A British organization dedicated to pressuring the public and government to recognize the existence and legitimacy of the childfree position.
www.kiddingaside.net

The Voluntary Human Extinction Movement

Saving the earth, one fewer person at a time.
www.vhemt.org

World Overpopulation Awareness

A one-stop shop for statistics, news, and other materials that support your earth-friendly lifestyle.
www.overpopulation.org

Eliminate Doubt

Child Substitute Adoption

The American Society for the Prevention of Cruelty to Animals can direct you to a child substitute adoption facility near you.
www.aspca.org

Potty Train Your Cat

This amazing Cat Seat makes potty training your feline child substitute easier.
www.catseat.com

Baby Think It Over

Find out how you can get your very own crying, pooping, barfing fake baby.
www.realityworks.com

Google Images

Look no further to search for horrifying images of birth and other child-related topics that will scare you sterile.
www.images.google.com

Photograph by Julian Cash

ABOUT THE AUTHOR

Jennifer L. Shawne is also the author of *Instant Weddings: From "Will You?" to "I Do!" in Four Months or Less,* published by Chronicle Books. She lives in San Francisco with her husband and two adorable feline child substitutes, Mim and Gita.

ABOUT THE ILLUSTRATOR

Anoushka Matus's illustrations appear regularly in numerous international magazines. She currently lives with her husband and son in Zurich, Switzerland.